Catholic Morality Revisited

Gerard S. Sloyan

CATHOLIC MORALITY REVISITED

ORIGINS AND CONTEMPORARY CHALLENGES

This book is for
Mary Perkins Ryan

Twenty-Third Publications
P.O. Box 180
185 Willow Street
Mystic CT 06355
(203) 536-2611

ISBN 0-89622-418-x
Library of Congress Catalog Number 89-51580

Scripture Index

These passages are the most important part of this book. Read and reflect on them, if you do nothing else.

Contents

Introduction

This book on Catholic morality is written for young people on their way to becoming adults and for those who teach them: parents, instructors in schools and schools of religion, preachers. There seems currently to be a vacuum in Catholic moral education. It follows on decades, even centuries, of earnest moralism. The young literally do not know what to do, not because no one has told them but because the tellers are themselves not sure of what things they should be telling. There is not enough firm conviction abroad about what the moral absolutes of Christians are and what things are relative to the circumstances. Parental living of the gospel is often in short supply. This makes it hard for the young to say that they are daily confronted by a consistent ethic within the church their parents are presumably committed to.

Prohibitions abound. That is not the problem. But often the prohibitions are not consistent with other patterns of permitted and prohibited behavior. The young are constantly being given mixed signals. They are frequently told what they should not do but not in a context of Christian liberty. This makes adherence to religious values seem to them a prison-house of the spirit. Patterns of conduct are put forward as "wrong" with little attempt to explain why they are wrong and what makes "right" to be right. Presenting any course of action as a matter of parental or school or church say-so is not likely to have much effect except in families where the Christian ethos is already in full possession. Even there, the outside influences are so great that a code of family behavior that goes critically unexamined cannot survive every storm or many storms.

Will a small book that argues cases with the reader, that tries to tell why certain patterns of human conduct have come to be identified as the gospel or Catholic way—two that in principle should be one—fare any better? That remains to be seen. One thing certain is that some teaching that gives reasons is better than no teaching. A second certainty is that a teaching that distinguishes between nuance in ethical dilemmas and open and shut cases is more likely to be taken seriously than one that knows no ambiguities. Life's hardest decisions tend to come at people in muddled circumstances. The courses of action most likely to be rejected are two: the one that is so clear that, upon being heard by a person of ill will, it will be turned down because of its clarity. The other is the course of action that cannot readily be acted on by a person of good will because of its lack of clarity. There are degrees of demand in all human conduct. They must be presented clearly.

The moral courses of action most likely to be followed are those that are based on an ideal like the life of integrity lived by Jesus, or those that promise the greatest happiness. The second is the ultimate motivating force in all that human beings do. It was the reason behind all the choices that Jesus made and proposed to others. Dante put it well centuries later (not that Jesus needed an interpreter) in a prayer to God: "In your will is our peace."

Catholics today who confess to an inability to agree with their church in all that it teaches are a commonplace. There have probably always been such, but this is a new era of independent judgment unencumbered by the facts. The facts, if explored carefully, might confirm the judgment of the individual Catholic. She (he) does not wish to act in accord with the consensus of the believing community. A decision has been made to act as one chooses, quite apart from either the body of Christ or any moral standard. This decision will be persisted in. Careful exploration might on the other hand have a different outcome. It could yield the conclusion that the course of action which attracts is morally valid by a Catholic standard. A person who has taken serious steps to formulate a good conscience may learn that there is more latitude within the body of believers than he or she had previously supposed. The alternative, of course, is to learn that there is less latitude, that a certain course of action is required or disallowed if one is to follow Christ and the gospel.

The chief conclusion erroneously arrived at in matters of Catholic morality is that there is some agency external to the individual labeled "the church" which acts as both legislator and censor to curb the individual's freedom. There is no such entity. The church is the congregation of the followers of Christ who mean to be his faithful disciples. It is made up of people and their pastors; of those who have had certain life experiences and those who have not; of some with more time for prayer and study and others with less; of persons with many cultural and ethical advantages and others with few. All in this community of faith have the vocation to be mutually supportive, the teachers among them at times the learners and vice versa. All are called to grow up in the Spirit to the full stature of Christ.

In this work of upbuilding, as Saint Paul called it, a few things can go seriously awry. There can be the "empty pulpit," a figure (and sometimes the fact) for the much-needed moral guidance that is not supplied by those with theological training. Parents can fail their children. Precepts can be laid down without the necessary reasons provided, or motives in the order of grace suggested. There can be short-term certitude expressed by teachers whose obligations as teachers are heavy and who do not have the patience to wait for the church's long-term judgment. Sometimes they intimate that they *are* the church. Settlements can be proposed with a view to the greatest good of the greatest number without regard to the demands of conscience on those who in certain situations fall outside a general precept. The pattern of conduct expected of all should be identified as such, while taking into account the individual cases that are not part of achieving the common good. In general, those who have a teaching office in the church express the Catholic consensus. They are safe guides in proposing the conduct that conforms to the will of God or does not. Like Jesus, they must be harsh with the impersonal imposers of burdens and clement toward the little ones who feel the weight.

Catholic morality is firm about those human problems that the children of Adam who are weak and sinful have wrestled with for centuries. It is, or ought to be, less sure of itself in some quite new human problems which a technical-industrial culture imposes. Firm answers are surely forthcoming but not until faithful people have lived with the challenges for some decades.

The rock that follows a pilgrim people on their journey is Christ. He is their one sure teacher and their guide. He will not fail them as the teachers and the taught seek to know God's will.

In the chapters to follow we will first examine how Jesus and the teachers of the apostolic age taught their disciples to behave: the gospel roots of Christian morality.

In sequence after that will come an exploration of when and how teachers of life in Christ first resorted for guidance to the philosophers who taught a "law of nature." A consideration of specific moral dilemmas will follow. Although any order of treatment should serve, Jesus' primary concern with greed as separating one from God recommends it for first place.

Next will be a consideration of the proper respect for oneself expressed by staying alive and staying well. The modern killers are alcohol, tobacco and other drugs, bad eating habits, stress, and carnage on the highway. One distortion of a healthy self-respect is an attitude that views body care and health as idols to be worshiped. This too will be examined.

Saint Paul called sexual deviation the only sin one could commit with one's body. This was an exaggeration, of course, but the principle behind it is important. We are not our own. We are the property of the Spirit. The right use of sex, then, will constitute the next consideration.

After that the topic will be "purity of heart," referring to Jesus' beatitude about the single-minded who avoid lying, cheating, and stealing—who, in brief, are true to their word. The final discussion will have to do with getting ahead in business without losing one's soul. It is not easy, as the dead souls of Christians spread around the landscape testify. Fidelity is made doubly difficult by the fact that the United States makes wars to protect its business interests, and the further fact that the manufacture of arms is so much a part of the national economy.

There will be a treatment of medical-moral problems in broad outline rather than detail. The same is true of moral dilemmas over the economy and the conduct of modern warfare. All three subjects are immense in scope. Some principles will be provided to help think about them, following which a little serious private reading will be indicated. Breadth and complexity is true of all that is so summarily discussed within these pages.

Some teachers, but especially parents, may be disappointed at the announcement that moral questions of such magnitude as these last-named are to be discussed. The immediate concern of parents is a report from the school that a teen-aged son is suspected of being a drug-user. Their daughter comes home from a high school party drunk or is found to be "on the pill." A son's dresser drawer accidently yields a well-hidden condom.

That these are the ways moral questions reach young and old alike cannot be doubted. Peer pressures are extremely influential. So are television programs, regular programming and cable equally, not to mention VCR films on which there is no control if they are available in someone else's home.

It will not be the business of this book to enter into the delicate question of confidence-building between parent and child. That is the subject of a special set of skills, hence another discussion. These pages will be concerned with what it is moral for the Catholic to do—parent and adolescent child equally—and what it is immoral to do. That should be task enough for one slim volume.

1

Catholic Morality: Distinctively Christian? Distinctively Catholic?

Writing about the conduct or behavior, the morality, of followers of Jesus Christ brings with it special responsibilities. It is important to get his teaching straight. He was, above all, the teacher of a way of living, of being fully human before God. To be a Christian is not so much a matter of believing in truths about God as of "doing the truth in love" (Ephesians 4:15). Christians believe that Jesus is the truth of God.

We live in a time when many who are baptized say they cannot "go along with" certain demands of Christian morality. They are in fact finding the centuries-old teaching of Jesus of Nazareth more than they can endure at this season of their lives. I mean to explore in these pages what is at the core of Christian morality and what are some more recent developments that may be described as not so central to gospel living as this core. I hope that this exploration will help readers clarify their ideas about what the demands of Christian morality actually are.

The discussions of what it means to be a disciple of Jesus Christ will explore whether there is a distinctively Christian morality and, if there is, whether Catholics have committed themselves at baptism to ways of conduct different from those of other Christians. The *motives* of behavior for a baptized believer will be looked into. So will the *means* available to do what one must do. How do God and Christ and the Spirit act as the teacher of humanity in the way it should go? What role do human teachers in the church play, like the pope and bishops and theologians? Is the analysis of nature and of nature's demands a requisite part of the divine teaching? If it is, how dependable are the results of such an analysis as a guide?

Questions of self-respect also have to be explored if Jesus' command to love our neighbor as ourself is to be obeyed. Faithful Christians in respecting their "selves," the gospel teaches, must be detached from possessions, respectful of their bodies, and obedient to the divine call.

How all this works out in the realms of honesty, truth-telling, chastity (the Christian's "good sex," not Dr. Ruth's or Phil Donahue's), life preservation, and care of the earth will be the subject of discussion in these pages. The avaricious, deceitful, lustful, rebellious person in all of us must be stripped away as we put on Christ. It can be done successfully only in the company of fellow Christians—or peers committed to the same morality, whatever their view of religion. It can be done intelligently only if we who are Christians know what we are bound to by our baptismal promises and why.

Many Cultures, Many Moralities

The Latin word *mos* (pl., *mores*) means "custom" or "practice." *Moralia* are habitual ways of doing things—right ways, it is to be hoped; wrong ways, it is to be feared. "Bad company corrupts good morals," old Menander said in his *Thaïs,* and Saint Paul picked that notion up as his comment on Isaiah's quotation of the immemorial watchword of the hedonist. That was the despairing"...'Let us eat and drink, for tomorrow we die'" (Isaiah 22:13; cf. 1 Corinthians 15:32–33).

A moralist is not a censorious busybody but a transmitter of the culture, one who reminds others how to live humanly and not as the beasts of the field. "This is our customary way of living, or should be," moralists say, "and these are the reasons for it."

A question that philosophical ethicists debate endlessly is whether there is one good or one best way to act humanly. They may use as their example truth-telling or fidelity to a marriage partner or doing justice. Most philosophers will have a favored teacher whose arguments they find convincing, such as Plato, Kant, Aristotle, or Nietzsche. They will follow this philosopher in determining what behavior most befits human beings, sometimes adding arguments of their own.

Religious people rely on a variety of saints and sages for guidance in the conduct of their lives. Some claim a divine revelation for the ethical code they adhere to with God as their teacher. Moses and the Hebrew prophets, Jesus Christ and the apostolic teaching, and the holy Qur'an delivered through Muhammad are claimed as intermediaries of the divine teaching. The nontheist ethics of the Buddha and the nonreligious ethics of Confucius may together, in fact, provide help to more people on the globe than any other code of behavior. Equally influential for millions are the ethics of Hinduism with its concept of Brahman and the various tribal codes that black Africans, Amerindians, and the Malay peoples are formed by, even though many of these peoples are at the same time Muslim or Christian.

Some philosophers, more venturesome than the rest, acquire data from cultural anthropology that lead them in another direction. They maintain not only that all behavior is learned but that in the course of the ages some peoples discover from their experience and teach their offspring a wide variety of moral imperatives.

Among these imperatives are the virtuous character of deceiving and killing the enemies of the people or the tribe; heterosexual sex-play among the young until they come to puberty; the approval, even the favored status, given to homosexuals and transvestites; promiscuity on certain ritual occasions or the offer of one's marriage partner as the greatest honor one can do a respected guest; and so on.

In brief, the point is made by anthropologists that just about any piece of behavior widely thought to be immoral is accepted as moral in some cultures. But the anthropologist at times fails to tell the whole story, getting it wrong through gullibility, ignorance of the language, or calculated deceit by the informants. Such was the case in Margaret Mead's study *Coming of Age in Samoa*, accepted for decades as a dependable report on sexual customs there when it was nothing of the sort. The whole story, the story that ought to be told, includes the tight controls, the unexpressed taboos, the limits beyond which behavior may *not* go even when it is going far beyond the limits familiar to the investigator.

Some nonreligious ethicists are not interested in those data about the moral limits imposed by each culture. That is because their chief concern is to establish the relative character of all human behavior. They were schooled in youth to accept the absolute moral character of certain human acts, often through a religious upbringing, and have later become apostles of moral flexibility or anarchy, and apostles in an evangelical mood at that. They want to tell the world that new freedoms are open to all because some on the globe have not heard of the restraints on freedom in the religious tradition in which they, the ethicists, were reared. But to use such data to target Christian morality is ill-founded, for certain of these restraints go back much farther than anything we know of from the Semitic and Greco-Roman patterns of morality that combined to produce the gospel morality for which Christianity claims a divine sanction.

The plain fact is that moralities differ around the globe even though human nature is much the same, if not in all particulars. Human nature is basically good and capable of heroic deeds in even the humblest of cultural circumstances. It is at the same time everywhere sinful and weak. Moralities differ because languages,

which are a part of culture, differ. Cultures in turn—strongly determined by their religious content—are many and varied. No
two peoples on the earth see all of life in quite the same way.

The East is dedicated to the moral value of "saving face" in a
way the West knows only by hearsay (although the *bella figura*
of Italy and the *honra* of the Iberian peninsula are its cousins).
Greek Christianity inherited *epieíkeia* (natural mildness, equity)
and *oikonomía* (orderly arrangement) from its pagan forebears. It
applies them in Christ's name in a way the Christian West finds
disturbingly lax. The Mediterranean and Celtic worlds have traditions of negotiating legal settlements in a way that the Anglo-
Saxon world cannot do, to the shock and surprise of all parties.
Amerindia, Asia, and Oceania all have moral codes of long standing which Christianity, in its zeal, has set at naught—often at its
peril.

Jewish morality and Christian morality have developed in importantly different ways, although in the first century—ritual
observance apart—they were identical. Different moral emphases in the Catholic, Orthodox, and Protestant worlds likewise
find their common roots in early Christianity. Black African morality in this country, first under siege by slavery and then by
the patterns of substandard living that resulted from slavery
and continue to this day, presents a paradigm of kinship family
loyalties that the white world scarcely knows.

Thus it should not surprise us that numerous approaches to
morality can be found in the Christian family of one and one
half billion people (893 million of them Catholic at last count)
with their wide varieties of culture. The outlooks on veracity
versus dissembling, individual versus communal rights, and
concern for the distribution of the world's goods versus almost
total unconcern are among the best examples of this diversity.

The Morality of the Earliest Church
The church of Jesus Christ came forth from the womb of Israel
teaching a way of human living that was at least as old as

Abraham. Abraham's way had derived from Babylonian understandings and was in turn refined by the code delivered by God to Moses. But the morality of the earliest church was not that of the patriarchs going back to the eighteenth century B.C.E. (Before the Common Era) or of those dating back to the conquest of Canaan in the twelfth-century. The way of living that the earliest Christians followed in society and individually drew not so much on the code attributed to the postexilic Judaite separatist Ezra (fifth century B.C.E.) as on the Greek or Hellenized Judaism of the Herodian era into which Jesus was born. Jesus' values were those of a Greek-influenced Jewish Palestine, as Paul's were of a Greek-influenced Jewish diaspora, both thoroughly biblical. Within fifty years of Jesus' death a group called the rabbis would pull back from anything smacking of Hellenist influence. But in the decades in which the tradition of Jesus came to birth, Judaism was very much Hellenized without experiencing any diminished fidelity to its God, the LORD.

Saint Paul, for example, provided lists of behaviors that no follower of Jesus might engage in. They were those that a Greek Stoic teacher of morals might just as well have provided. Paul writes:

It is obvious what proceeds from the flesh: lewd conduct [*porneía*], impurity, licentiousness, idolatry [a peculiarly Jewish sin, although some pagan philosophers abhorred it equally], sorcery, hostilities, bickering, jealousy, outbursts of rage, selfish rivalries, dissensions, factions, envy, drunkenness, orgies, and the like...(Galatians 5:19–21).

This is a rather intimidating list, taken all in all. Paul presents it as the way of *sárx*, that is, the "flesh" or the old eon. Life in Christ allowed none of this behavior, just as the new *pneûma* (Spirit) had as its fruit "...love, joy, peace, patient endurance, kindness, generosity, faith, mildness, and chastity..." (vv. 22–23). The point is that Paul could have taught these lists to Jewish proselytes equally well in his Pharisee days, influenced as the

Judaism of his day was by certain Greek values. In Paul's message, it was not the content of a life of vice or virtue that had changed for the Christian from a parent Israel but only the means and the motives. It was the Spirit of Christ dwelling in the baptized that made the new life achievable and provided them with the will to accomplish it.

Mark's gospel has Jesus explaining to his disciples that a divorcing man (i.e., one who in Jewish custom dismisses his wife unilaterally) who remarries, commits adultery against the first wife, "and the woman who divorces her husband and marries another commits adultery" (Mark 10:12). The latter warning is almost unthinkable as a teaching of Jesus to fellow Jews in his lifetime. Jewish divorce was a writ of dismissal by a husband. It had no female equivalent. But among pagans and a few prosperous, nonobservant Jews, divorce was a legal possibility in the empire for both sexes. That is why it could appear as part of the moral code of a religious community that had increasing numbers of non-Jews (see also 1 Corinthians 7:13).

Jesus as a Jewish Teacher

The precise morality of the Palestinian communities that believed in Jesus as Christ and risen Lord is not known. That is because there are no records of those Aramaic-speaking churches. The general character of this morality can be deduced, however, from the four gospels, which had their roots though not their growth in Palestine.

Jesus was a familiar type of Jewish teacher whose thrust we surely know. He was a Pharisee in general outlook (on the resurrection of the body, for example) but apparently not warm toward the Pharisees' complete separatism from other Jews in matters of ritual purity. He was more inclined to the school of Hillel than of Shammai. If he departed from Jewish moral teaching in any particular, we do not know it. We do know that he favored mercy over justice as both occur in the biblical tradition, without ever presenting God as disinterested in justice. He took the side of his rigorist contemporaries—the school of Shammai—in the matter of easy divorce by men. He was even stricter than they in his unequivocal opposition to divorce as practiced by the Jewish men of his day.

Jesus supported completely, so far as we can determine, the written Torah and the morality of the prophetic and the wisdom writings. No tradition of support, however, for the then emerging "oral Torah" gathered around his name, with the possible exception of coupling biblical tenets like those on love of God and love of neighbor (Deuteronomy 6:5 and Leviticus 19:18). This could mean either that he disfavored the concept of oral Law or that when the evangelists wrote up his teachings in the gospels fifty years later, they suppressed any support of it Jesus might have expressed.

In fact, the Jesus movement in Hellenist Judaism was never *halakhic* (walking in the "path" of the precepts) but always radically biblical. It bore a relation in some particulars to the morality of fringe groups like the Essenes. Jesus' teaching on the way to live as his disciples comes to us as depending solely on the Scriptures and his interpretation of them. This is probably because the ever-increasing influx of non-Jews into the church relieved it of the problem of how to live as late first-century Jews were living. The two patterns of behavior were close, but already they were not identical.

We shall be looking into the content of the morality of Jesus and his first-century disciples in the chapters that follow. Suffice it to say that the Jewish Scriptures as interpreted by the teacher Jesus gave those early believers all the guidance they needed. The Jews were not a speculative people. They did not explore the motives of human acts as Plato might, or means and ends in the manner of Aristotle. The question of why it was good to be good and evil to be evil did not detain them. The common folk among the Jews would have said it was self-evident because their God was holy. The idea of holiness would have included that which was ethically demanding, but the distinction would probably have been lost on ordinary Jews. Their all-holy God simply demanded that the people Israel live this way, quite un-like the surrounding pagans.

The learned Jew, in other words, would have given the will of an all-holy God as the reason that good was good and evil evil. The Lord's commandments made it so. If you had attributed to the Jews of that time a voluntaristic image of God, they would have acknowledged this cheerfully. The intrinsic rightness of the ethical act is never discussed in the Christian Scriptures or the rabbinic literature. If the Jewish teachers of the period, being highly intelligent men, had been faced with the proposition that the ten commandments were ten convenient headings under which to group all that contributes to human well being, they would have agreed. Both horizontally, at the human level, and vertically, in relation to God, these precepts would have been praised as ten basic ways to preserve the image of God in hu-manity. But the early rabbis would never have initiated a discus-sion about those terms. They knew that obedience to the divine commands would result in the maximum of well-being ("peace"), both for the people of Israel corporately and for all its members. The "ten words" were holy because they were the ones the Lord had chosen for Israel to live by.

The Uniqueness of Jesus' Teaching

Jesus did more than assume and teach the prevailing morality of his Jewish people. He featured its noblest elements in a combi-nation that can only be considered remarkable. Forgiveness of enemies, love of neighbor as the essential concomitant of the love of God, and compassion for the poor, the downtrodden, and society's outcasts can all be found in the rich treasury of biblical teaching and rabbinic commentary on it. The marvel was that Jesus brought these many strands together at so early a time in the rabbinic tradition that came to be called Judaism.

Some say of Jesus ungenerously that he taught nothing new, nothing that was not in the tradition. That is an apologetic re-mark directed not so much against him as against those ignorant

of the tradition, namely, most Christians. If there were no Jew-
ish-Christian struggle of twenty centuries, this type of defensive
remark would not surface. David Flusser of the Hebrew University of Jerusalem comes close to the mark when he says of the
teacher of Galilee:

> It is clear that Jesus' approach to God and [humanity]...is
> unique and incomparable. According to the teachings of
> Jesus you have to love the sinners, while according to
> Judaism you have not to hate the wicked. It is important to
> note that the positive love even toward enemies is Jesus'
> personal message. We do not find this doctrine in the New
> Testament outside of the words of Jesus himself....In
> Judaism hatred is practically forbidden, but love to the
> enemy is not prescribed.[1]

Proverbs 25:21-22 does in fact instruct one to give food and
drink to one's enemy, thus heaping "live coals...on his head"
and winning the Lord's vindication. But, as Flusser says, Jesus
took the teaching further. For example, the teacher of Nazareth
regarded all possessions as a threat to true piety. For him mammon, or the exaggerated devotion to *things*, was an obstacle to
virtue.

In the manner of the Essenes of Qumrân, Jesus taught that a
servant of God should be "a messenger of Thy goodness; that to
the humble he might bring glad tidings of Thy great mercy...and
everlasting joy to those who mourn."[2] Jesus was in every respect
committed to the poor and the outcast, the sorrowful and the
deprived. He never had a kind word to say for the rich or the
hoarding of possessions, even among the poor.

There was, then, a distinctively Christian morality from the
start, if by that is understood a Jewish morality featuring certain
emphases. To debate whether Jesus was an absolute innovator is
ultimately fruitless. He was by any reckoning a divinely sent re-
vealer of God and the author of a tradition in human behavior
that featured the best in Jewish biblical and postbiblical morality.

Christians view him as God's "only Son," which augments the authority of his teaching by an infinity but does not change its content. The four evangelists capture Jesus' moral teaching in sayings that each of them selected from other collections of his statements. They do the same in the parables which, like the sayings they possessed, they altered to suit their contexts. Jesus' instruction comes to us in heavily edited versions but its force, for all that, is little diminished. It is, if anything, enhanced.

The New Testament teachers other than the evangelists were also inheritors of Jesus' Spirit. One cannot find a moral demand in Paul that is dissonant from the demands of Jesus. (A nuanced difference is Paul's decision that the believer is "not bound" if the unbeliever wishes to "separate," i.e., divorce [1 Corinthians 7:15]. Jesus is not recorded as having a view on divorce that involved pagans.) The same consistency with Jesus' ethics is true of the remaining writers of epistles and the books known as Hebrews and Revelation. Even though these writers lack the stark rhetorical force of Jesus' Hebraic speech, and were at times a little "pat" in the ordered church universe they sought to create (see the epistles to Timothy and Titus), they could not keep the vigor of this awesome moralist from shining through.

Jesus taught, like a man of his people, that God has given to human creatures the power to choose the good and reject the evil. There was for him no debating whether humanity is free. He took it as axiomatic that it is. Saint Paul opted for recourse to the gift of the Spirit dwelling within those who believe in Christ's resurrection as the motive force that makes fidelity to the law of Christ possible. Like any Jew, he was convinced of humanity's basic freedom. Paul's view of conscience became a Christian inheritance. His word for it is *syneídēsis*, found in the Septuagint translation of Job 27:6 (a cognate word) and Qoheleth 10:20. It is better translated "consciousness," and is the capacity to judge one's own actions, either in retrospect, or in prospect. The word occurs thirty times in the New Testament, fourteen of them in 1 Corinthians and Romans. Paul relates conscience to the gift of the Spirit in Romans 9:1, much as his discussion of the Spirit's action in us had done in 8:9, 16, 26. In 14:23 he says that whatever is done not out of faith, meaning good faith, is sin.

Paul's many brief paeans to the power of God's grace have led some Christians to put a low value on human liberty. But close inspection of his teaching reveals that grace only enhances and enlarges freedom. Grace does nothing to inhibit or diminish freedom, least of all to destroy it. At one point Paul identifies as sin all human choice made apart from Christ—that is, on the basis of human resources alone (see Romans 14:23). But free choice made in Christ is unequivocally good.

A caricature of Paul's salutary reminder of the perils of freedom has described the human will as weak to the point of incapacity. Jesus would be shocked at this development. For him as a Jew the power to choose was a great gift of God to creatures. More divine assistance could be given, but none that threatened the original gift. Jesus never wrestled with the problems that come with being a free but sinful human as Paul did. Yet in Romans 7:13–25 Paul is not correctly understood when he is read as a tormented victim of conscience. There he is a soliloquizer for Everyperson, crying out as if to say in a commonplace of human experience: "It is hard to be moral. Have you not known the pull within you?" Jesus might have praised Paul's performance but given a gentle warning of the possibility of its being misconstrued. Paul's reflection on the struggle to do the right was badly understood in various ages of Christian anxiety.[3] Some even erroneously took him to be saying that God's commandments were impossible of fulfillment. Jesus never invited people to anguished ethical debate. His teaching was more like, "Search out what is right and *do* it."

Second-Century Developments

When the few of the second-century Christian writers (the "sub-apostolic age") whose works are extant employed the materials that ended up in the gospels, they featured Jesus' short, pithy axioms more than his stories. The Pauline letters likewise featured axiomatic ethical teaching. The concluding paraenetic sections (from the word for "advice" or "encouragement") of these epistles became an arsenal of moral counsel and command. Later, instructions on what to do and what not to do were often assembled and linked together without the reasons first alleged by Jesus and Paul that had given them meaning. Later—much later—there came to be a body of Christian ethical teaching that derived from the philosophers and was all but cut off from its roots in the two testaments of Scripture.

The main motive provided by Jesus for right action was that obedience to God would fulfill the human vocation, which consisted in doing God's will. Preparing for entry into God's rule ("kingship") at the end of this age was another strong motive that Jesus put forward. Paul proposed being "in Christ" or being fitting "members" of his body—the body of glory now with God—as the chief reason for believers to conform to the Christian way of life. It was not a demand imposed from without by "the church" (although Paul was quite happy to show that this dynamic motive had mothered numerous local churches). This way of living was a demand of the spirit dwelling within believers, crying out to God's Spirit as the two recognized each other. "Be all that you can be" is something that Paul would have approved—not as Operation Bootstrap but as a description of the call of the Spirit to the baptized to permit their fulfillment by the same Spirit.

Again, some second-century apologists summarized the morality of the first-century apostolic writings in ways such as lists of virtues and vices suitable for memorization by candidates for baptism. In this technique something important was lost. The wonders of the grace-life featured by Paul seemed in one case, the First Epistle of Clement, to yield to little more than a call to emulate the heroes of the Jewish Scriptures, even though that writer knew Paul's teaching that justification was a gift of God. Commandments of the "law of Christ" were often presented apodictically without much discussion.

Of this period we do not know which of the biblical and apostolic writings were selected for the weekly assembly, nor how
they were developed orally. Neither do we have baptismal homilies of the sort that marked a later time—although many students of the canonical writings think that the First Epistle of Peter and Colossians were such homilies. The anonymous Second
Epistle of Clement, sometimes called the first post-New Testament sermon, puts matters succinctly when it says:

> You must realize that our stay in this world of the flesh is
> slight and short, but Christ's promise is great and wonder-
> ful, and means rest in the coming kingdom and in eternal
> life. What, then, must we do to get these things, except to
> lead a holy and upright life and to regard these things of
> the world as alien to us and not to desire them? For in
> wanting to obtain these things we fall from the right way.
> The Lord says, "No servant can serve two masters." If we
> want to serve both God and money, it will do us no good.
> "For what good does it do a person to gain the whole
> world and forfeit his life?" This world and the world to
> come are two enemies. This one means adultery, corrup-
> tion, avarice and deceit, while the other gives them up. We
> cannot, then, be friends of both. To get the one we must
> give the other up....If [Noah and Job and Daniel] cannot
> save their children by their uprightness, what assurance
> have we that we shall enter God's kingdom if we fail to
> keep our baptism pure and undefiled? Or who will plead
> for us if we are not found to have holy and upright deeds?
> (5:5-6:9)[4]

This selection should help to make clear the second-century
shift in interest from this world to the next, which is not quite
the "world that is to come" of an apocalyptic Jewish church. Jesus' demand that no one or nothing in life be preferred to the
rule of God was subtly transformed into a despising of the this-
worldly as if it were by definition corrupt. The Gnostic and

Docetic threats were hovering low in this period. The church escaped them, but barely.

Part of this "near miss" was the Jewish teaching, which the church inherited, that sex should be engaged in by the married for the begetting of children only, not for mere pleasure as was thought to be the case with pagans. Second marriage even after a partner's death came to be frowned on by influential teachers like Tertullian, going back to the second-century Plea of Athenagoras, who was alone in calling it adulterous. It was never prohibited outright.

With the third and fourth centuries came the influence of Stoicism—a daughter of Platonism—which categorized all passion as unworthy of the higher human spirit. The "carnals" might yield to passion—all the passions, not just that of sex—but the "spirituals" had to rise above it. *Apátheia* was the ideal, a passionless existence. This nonbiblical outlook became very influential, as we shall see.

Christian morality was taught to adult candidates for baptism largely out of the wisdom books of the Bible (the "Writings"). Because the church early became so gentile in make-up, a distinction was developed that no Jew would have recognized—namely, between the ethical and the ritual requirements of the Mosaic Law. The former bound the Christian, it was said; the latter did not. Which ethical prescriptions of the Law did and did not bind was a matter of the Christians' deciding that particular ethical precepts did not apply to them because they were not culturally Jewish. Examples would be the allowance of multiple wives, the "law of the brother-in-law" governing the transmission of property, and, much later, a change in the degree of consanguinity required for incest.

In any case, the declaration of some that the church cannot sanction this matter or that because the law of God does not allow it rings hollow when it is discovered that many of the early church's decisions were arrived at with a sense of sovereign freedom. Like the rabbis, the bishops and theologians of the church (often the same people) decided what was the perceived

will of God. Their interpretations of the Bible became (and become) Christian morality.

Morality Preached and Decreed

For a dozen centuries, Christian morality was what was
preached as Christian morality: in the sermons of bishops at the
rite of initiation, in the commentaries of the church fathers on
the Scriptures, above all in the West in the moral compendium
of Pope Saint Gregory I ("the Great"), who figuratively sat on
Augustine's shoulders. The latter writing, *Moralia in Job*, a commentary in thirty-five books, is sometimes called the first handbook of moral theology. Augustine and Gregory above all others in the West place in some doubt contemporary warning to
heed the teaching of the church but disregard the opinions of
theologians. It was the opinions of these two authors *as theologians* that became the teaching of the church (e.g., on original sin
and purgatory).

Some ethical matters were settled by imperial decree, as when
the Eastern emperor decided that Matthew 5:32 and 19:9 were
true clauses of exception that permitted the injured partner to
remarry after divorce resulting from adultery. The Western legislation—imperial, not specifically church, but they were reckoned as the same—decided differently, as is well known. This
was centuries before the schism of 1045 and the years immediately following. Similarly, the West came to allow unlimited
marriages after the deaths of spouses, frowning on them faintly
even as it did so, while the Eastern churches settled on four marriages and no more, however the spouses were serially dis-
patched.

The canonists of the twelfth century in the papal chair were
influential in making the settlements of Roman public law into
church law. It was a period when no civil authority existed to
record effectively births, marriages, or deaths. Neither could
such authority pass on the validity of unions or the legitimacy of
children. The church's sacramental life was thoroughly

entwined with people's civic lives, the assumption being that to become a Christian at baptism and a member of the political order or state were the same thing.

Protestant versus Catholic Morality

The Reformers repudiated the above understanding. They identified the sacraments—which they reckoned as two or three, matrimony not among them—as acts of faith, not civil actions. At the same time they sought to disengage the gospel from any juridical ties. The result was a bifurcation of Christian morality into distinct Protestant and Catholic expressions. The former sought New Testament warrant for all Christian behavior and the resolution of troubled consciences by justifying faith alone. European Catholics, for their part, continued in the same line as previously in their preaching and confessional practice. They too believed that faith alone justified but they sought to learn its ethical demands, as before, from the church's tradition on the virtues and the vices. Repentance of sin was necessary if there was to be a return to grace and a public reconciliation with the community.

By the time of the Reformation, Catholic preaching and practice had become influenced to some degree by St. Thomas Aquinas's adaptation of Aristotle's *Ethics* in his *Summary of Theology*, part 2. This recourse yielded a moral theory based on the mean between excess and defect as applied to the three theological and the four cardinal virtues. A theory of natural law, which St. Thomas developed from his teacher St. Albert of Cologne, was part of the ethics of the Scholastics, but it was not very influential at the popular level. Confessors' handbooks were. These contained lists of sins against the decalogue, the twofold commandment of love, and the precepts of the church. This same material was being preached throughout the Middle Ages in a tradition going back to the lists compiled by men like St. Isidore of Seville (d. 636).

The confessional practice of medieval Europe brought into

being a distinctive Catholic morality that went largely untouched by the Reformation. The *ethos* of Orthodox and Protestant Christians, needless to say, was unaffected by this development.

Eighteenth-century Catholic life in the West witnessed the much-maligned case method (or "casuistry"), in which hypothetical problems of conscience were resolved for the guidance of confessors. The solutions had the merit of maintaining that circumstances drastically alter cases, often reducing the possibility of formal sin to the zero level. Casuistry's high point was the triumph of "probabilism" over a variety of both more rigorous and laxer moral systems. This school of moralists maintained that the probable opinion of any respected (because learned) theologians could safely be followed for the resolution of one's troubled conscience. It provided relief to scrupulous millions, both penitents and confessors.

Interestingly and importantly, the twenty-one ecumenical councils (as the Catholic West reckons them) almost never dealt with moral questions. (The sole exceptions were some medieval declarations made in favor of marriage, sex, and childbearing against heretics called the Cathars or Albigenses, and the pastoral teachings of Vatican II's *Gaudium et Spes* ["The Church in the Modern World"].) Spelling out what the law of the gospel required was the province of theologians. It was their consensus views on interest-taking, theft, abortion, and a host of other matters that prevailed. From the Middle Ages onward popes sought the opinions of theologians at universities like Oxford, Cambridge, and Paris to resolve disputed cases—except for those popes who sought no one's counsel on anything, like Boniface VIII.

Beginning with the mid-nineteenth century, there was a new development. The pope emerged as the supreme theologian of Western Catholicity. Previously he had been only its supreme canonist and arbiter, although the faith of the Roman See was always required as part of a consensus settlement of bishops on the teaching of the church. This fairly recent development in the role of the pope has been marked by the proliferation of papal

encyclical letters since the time of Pius IX (1846–1878). The inno-
vation peaked with the demand that Pope Paul VI placed upon
his fellow bishops in 1965 that they disregard the moral problem
attending contraception in their pastoral constitution *Gaudium et
Spes*. He was to address the subject himself in an encyclical letter
of July 1968 (*Humanae Vitae*). Declaring papal teaching superior
to churchwide episcopal teaching had its seeds in Vatican I. Pius
IX knew that he needed a vote on the question of papal (as distinct from church) infallibility. He asked for it and, despite the
many misgivings of the bishops who stayed in Rome for the
vote, he got it.

This brings us to the present age in Catholic morality, when
the incumbent pope is acknowledged in practice as not only the
chief but the sole teacher in moral matters. Whether he teaches
as the voice of Catholic consensus of his fellow bishops (the "ordinary magisterium"), of theologians, or of the faithful is something not easy to discover in certain areas, chiefly those touching
on sexuality. Recent popes have not let the question be raised.

They have called their teaching, delivered either in person or
through curial theologians speaking for them, official Catholic
teaching. It *is* that because of the high office they hold. It is usually traditional Catholic morality, but sometimes it does not
have a very long history as such.

Papal teaching can always be followed as a safe guide to action. Recent popes have reckoned its binding force even higher
than that by declaring that, in moral matters, it cannot be departed from without sin. This teaching constitutes a hardship for
those who, like the married of well-developed conscience, con-
clude that to follow papal teaching in certain specific matters is
something their consciences do not allow. This is an unenviable
position for any Catholic to be in, whether pope or parent.

It is not always easy to know where moral truth lies, let alone
act on it. Our moral judgments can be clouded. There can be ignorance, but also, as Aquinas puts it, a "misdirected will or love
arising in society or in individuals out of sin." In our day this
deflected will is likely to arise out of the conviction that one

enjoys perfect autonomy of decision. Despite this possibility of error through ignorance or self-will, conscience may never be gone against. It must always be acted on once every effort has been made to form a right conscience. God may know that the choice is objectively wrong, but the earnest Catholic seeking to do God's will has not been able to discover the error. Such a one would be morally culpable if he or she were not to perform the act. The question all must face at the judgment is whether they did all in their power to act in good conscience.

2

Jesus
and the
Apostolic Teachers

When Jackie Gleason died in 1987, a newspaper observed that "the man who was afraid to die did." The seventy-one-year-old, Manhattan-born comedian made no secret of his apprehension at the prospect of judgment. In a segment of "60 Minutes" that was filmed well before his death but screened not long before it, Gleason was pressed by the journalist Morley Safer on the subject of judgment, although not in those words. The television-viewing public—which can hear about a fundamentalist heaven and hell by the hour any time it wishes—was treated to a few minutes of sober reflection on the justice and mercy of God directed toward the sins of a lifetime. It does not entertain these sentiments often.

Gleason's response was not expressed in theological language, but older Catholics recognized in his words the oblique expression of the faith of their youth. He put a few matters in the subjunctive case, making "ifs" out of them. He knew he could not assume his own beliefs in 20 million viewers, or even in his questioner. But he gave every indication he took very seriously the phrase, "He will come to judge the living and the dead," and hoped he had nothing to fear.

The expectation of final judgment used to be the outlook of all Europe, Jewish and Christian. The American frontier, sporadically evangelical as it was, by and large held the same conviction. The new waves of immigrants reinforced it. People worried about their sins in an earlier American day, and at death, even under the hangman's noose, they repented. More recently, though—since World War I or thereabouts—Christianity began to be viewed by novelists and popular pundits and semi-educated instructors in colleges and universities as a huge guilt-producing machine, a corporate superego that told basically good people, "It is wrong because you want to do it." The Christian faith became, in the popular mind, the inventor of sin. Up to that point it had enjoyed a reputation as a practitioner of how to deal with sin. There is such a thing as Jewish sin and guilt—not identical with its Christian counterpart but closely allied to it. But that is another story.

Catholic Morality: A Treasure, Not a Burden

One meets not a few Catholics nowadays who laugh nervously, even a little apologetically, when they confess to having a problem with their consciences. They say, "It must be my Catholic upbringing." This could be a tragic situation: not knowing the difference between false guilt, a confusion that can cause psychic damage, and true guilt, a reality of the soul that can be eliminated by repentance. Are we becoming a Catholic people that, instead of glorying in healthy consciences sensitive to good and evil, apologizes for them? A tender conscience is not a social embarrassment. For Catholics it is a sign that the moral expectations Jesus has of his friends are being taken with utmost seriousness.

Jesus never spoke of God as someone who lay in wait to trap the unwary. The God he called "my Father" was not someone distressed when human beings took a little joy out of life. Jesus, like any Jew, thought that life had a purpose. He knew that the choices we make have consequences, serious consequences. They affect us and those all around us. God at the judgment, being just, cannot do anything but honor the freedom that was the original divine gift to us.

Catholic morality is simply the following of Jesus Christ, neither more nor less. It is the awareness that to be human is to live in God's image, distorted in us by the sin of all the ages but potentially restored in us by grace. The only perfect realization of that image is the man of Nazareth, the world's redeemer. Jesus' interpretation of the teachings of the Jewish Scriptures about how to be children of our Father in heaven is *the* dependable teaching on how to fulfill that image. The teaching is embodied in his person.

To be human is to live with what may seem in youth to be infinite possibilities. They are hampered, however, by a cosmic alienation that puts us out of joint with our original destiny. Every one of the world's peoples has wrestled with the mystery of humanity's unfulfilled condition. St. Paul called it "sin" (not the same thing as "sins," his word for which we translate "transgressions"). Paul personified sin in a powerful myth, setting against it the Christ who took its measure. His Epistle to the Romans needs to be read with care on all this, chapter 7 beginning at verse 5 in particular.

St. Augustine, who was probably not a Punic Semite but of European stock, was not thoroughly at ease with biblical categories. He reduced the tragic myth of human beginnings in Genesis to merely historical proportions. This gave Christians of the West a legacy that has been a puzzle to them ever since. Western Christians have often viewed "original sin" (Augustine's name for hereditary guilt, the "origin" being our personal human beginnings) not as the mystery of the human tendency to evil, but as a problem in justice. "Why should I be penalized," they ask, "because Adam and Eve chose to...?" and so on. To think this way, in terms of a historical human pair, is to miss the history that matters most. All the generations on the earth since the start, who have freely rebelled against God in imitation of the couple in the Eden account, provide the history that is the center of gravity here. Saint Paul was interested, above all, in the one man of history who reversed the trend. Jesus was the anointed of God who lived as all humans should—God-like, honest and obedient. He was free of the burden of "sin" and, in consequence, sins.

Jesus took on our burden voluntarily. He "became sin for us" (2 Corinthians 5:21). But he never for a moment in his own person rebelled against God.

Is it possible to live a life of thorough human goodness as Jesus did or did God constitute him uniquely free from sin? The second answer is "yes" but that does not make the first one "no." Christian faith holds that "despite the increase of sin, grace has far surpassed it." That is Paul's poetic way of saying (Romans 5:20) that the favor God shows us in Christ far outruns the power of sin over us. In baptism we have received "the overflowing grace and gift of justice [righteousness]," in virtue of which we are called to "live and reign through...Jesus Christ" (Romans 5:17). Reconstituted in his image, we are called to a life of moral goodness. We are called to more than that, to the holiness of godhead itself.

The tradition of the Reformation stresses the continuing power of sin over us if we do not trust the grace of Christ. The Orthodox and Catholic traditions emphasize not only the overcoming of sin by grace but also the possibility of living as members of a holy church. Although all are sinners, each of us is able to live a life unmarred by grievous sin if we let the Spirit's power prevail in us. Catholic morality features the divine goodness in humans as creatures of God and the divine possibilities open to them as a redeemed creation. Human redemption is a divine gift but it is a thoroughly human affair. It was achieved for us by one of us.

To trust in human power alone is the sin of presumption. To capitulate to the power of evil is the sin of despair. The golden mean of Christian morality is to act on the conviction, in faith, that because God has recreated us in the image of Christ, lives of thoroughgoing human integrity are possible. Onlookers, both fellow believers and others, should see in mature Christian adults a company of "saints." Such is the designation that Christians of the apostolic age unashamedly gave themselves because of what God had done for them. Modern "sainthood" seems to come in two kinds—the total self-confidence by which people think they have done and can do no wrong, and the nervous anxiety that they can do no right. Neither of the two is the pattern of Christian holiness revealed in the Scriptures. They are cruel caricatures. Only when believers follow the pattern of Scripture (a pattern that is often placed beyond recognition by inauthentic interpretations of it) will they have the moral teaching of their Catholic tradition straight.

A Corporate Morality

Jesus was primarily a teacher of the way people ought to act, not of the way they ought to believe. He was a Jew, a man of the Bible. He took for granted belief in the one God and Israel's covenanted calling.

As to human conduct—what the Greeks called ethics—Jesus' concern was chiefly with the behavior of his people as a people. He conducted himself like a reformer of Israel and would have said willingly, "Such is my vocation." He recalled his Jewish people to the obligations of their corporate, covenanted life. They knew the challenge. It was the only one that God had issued to them through Abraham, Moses, and all the prophets: to be a holy *people.*

Nothing was changed in that challenge for those who followed Jesus. The disciples whom Jesus summoned—not just the Twelve but the dozens and the hundreds who followed him closely—were to be a shining light that could not be hidden, just

as Israel's ancient calling was (and is) to be "a light to the nations." It was implicitly understood that individuals make up
the Jewish people. Jesus, however, who in his own person *was*
the gospel, addressed himself to them only in terms of their peoplehood. In the same way, the gospel is addressed to us who believe in it not as individuals but in our peoplehood, in our life as
the church.

The concept of peoplehood is very hard to grasp and harder
still to live by. The culture we live in is so atomized that each of
us is daily thrown on his or her resources in a cruel way. There
is a widespread understanding that ours is an autonomy in decision making. This is not only not the case in the order of reality,
but it also would be impossible to exercise that type of autonomy even if we were to have it. Even as believers we cannot
count on religious peoplehood to sustain us. A thousand messages a day are beamed at us that say, "You're on your own and
don't forget it." And we believe these messages. We do well to
do so because, unfortunately, the larger Catholic community
acts as if it were so.

The problem is not new. Extreme individualism in the West is
as old as the Renaissance. Put it at five hundred years, with far
older roots. The form it takes in religion is that the Christian
Scriptures, which were addressed corporately to Israel, a part of
which became the church, are heard individually. The culture
around us, which is individualist in orientation, has simply prevailed.

The negative influence of individualism in religion surfaces in
other ways. Some Christian teachers have asserted that although
God spoke to the Jews as a people, a drastic change occurred
with Christ, in whom God began to address the individual human heart. Beginning with Augustine one hears sentiments like
the following:

I desire to know God and the soul.
Q. Nothing more?
A. Absolutely nothing. (*Soliloquies* 2.7)

This is a woeful betrayal of the Christian tradition. It is clear from the gospels that Jesus was a great lover of persons. So too, presumably, were Hillel and Ezra and all the prophets who preceded them. In fact, no change of direction occurred, as an attentive listening to the books of the New Testament will reveal. It would help, perhaps, if the pronoun "you" in English had a plural form distinct from the singular as it does in Greek. That is because all of Jesus' admonitions were addressed to his people as a people. But the problem is theological rather than grammatical. It stems from a tragic downgrading of Jewish solidarity by Christians as part of their praise of Christian "universalism." This is compounded by a heretical emphasis on the church as an assembly of those individually "saved" rather than as the corporate communion of saints under the headship of Christ, an understanding featured in the epistles to the Colossians and Ephesians.

Whatever its roots, this quite unbiblical individualism has as firm a grip on Catholics as on any Christians. The "fundamentalists" are a special case. Among these conservative evangelicals, as some prefer to be called, it flourishes above all. The corporate morality of the New Testament has perhaps been best retained by the communions in the free church tradition. I refer to those that think of themselves as a "peculiar people" in the mold of the apostolic age and for that reason countercultural: Mennonites, the Amish, and various Brethren churches. The Latter-day Saints, an offshoot of Christianity, are by all means rightly praised for their corporate ethos of the family, which is a biblical heritage.

The tragedy for Christians is that the Christian ethos is often more readily recognized by those outside a given Christian community than by those within it. Catholics in England were the people who did not divorce to marry again, as any faithful reader of Agatha Christie's mystery stories can discover. Irish Catholic servant girls were favored by the propertied Yankees of the northeastern United States because they did not steal ("had to tell it in confession" was the convenient explanation). Hiring

Americans of Portuguese Catholic stock or African-American Jehovah's Witnesses as domestics is favored in some parts of this country "because they're honest." Surely other ethnic families can be singled out for similar praise. The point is, a corporate Christian identity and corresponding code of conduct are maintained. The same cannot be said, unhappily, of the larger communions or of Catholics generally.

The Privatization of Morality

Although a sense of corporate morality does survive among some Christian groups, it is not now the uppermost consideration of most churches. "The church of your choice" has been readily translated into "the morality of your choice" because the two concepts of freedom are so closely allied. In the civil sphere the privacy of the individual has been elevated to the status of a constitutional right and to the point that it threatens the public good ("common weal"). The protection of the individual lives of the safely born has been able to prevail in our culture to the detriment of the protection of our corporate life. As regards the very young, it is cause for satisfaction that the rights of women have not yet been claimed over the rights of their children, although that may come. The public as a public, not just a religious people as a people, is vulnerable before the claims made for the all-sovereign individual. A discouraging result of this privatization of morality is that one does not readily say: "Well, she couldn't have perjured herself. She is a Catholic," as one might say, "He couldn't have been drunk. He is a Muslim."

No one can make the case that Jesus and the apostolic church were disinterested in individuals, hence in their individual rights. The church in any age can never be disinterested in individuals' rights. The thrust of the New Testament is that Christian conduct is always primarily the behavior, individual and social, of people who belong to a holy community. For Jesus this community was Israel, for the next generations Israel and the gentiles who associated themselves with a movement directed to the restoration of Israel. By the early second century it had become a gentile community. The church, however large it grows, like the mustard bush with its nesting birds (Matthew 13:32; see Ezekiel 17:23), must always be a reproach to the world, to the birds not in its branches. It must give guidance by the uprightness of its corporate life. If this is elitism (see "the elect" of Mark 13:27; Luke 18:7), it is an elitism of the masses.

The Morality Jesus Taught

Jesus did not speculate about human conduct. Like the God of heaven who had offered a covenant to Israel, it was for him a given. His hearers knew how they should act because the God of Israel was their teacher through Moses. The commandments they received were largely apodictic, which is to say absolutely certain and capable of clear demonstration (e.g., "You shall not commit adultery" [Exodus 20:14]). This is not the same as being arbitrary. Some others were casuistic (e.g., "If [the case should be that] in the open fields...a man comes upon such a betrothed maiden..." [Deuteronomy 22:25]). Jesus' hearers grew up instructed in how a faithful Jew should act. They knew what lying and rape and theft were. They had before their eyes an ideal that admitted none of this aberrant behavior, namely, that of the "just" in Israel. They also had a few ugly examples of opposite behavior, like the incestuous Herod Antipas (Mark 6:17) and the corrupt high priesthood of the temple (appointed by Herod the Great and the Caesars).

Jesus' hearers were not so simple-minded as to think that there were no complex moral cases of ownership or false witness or claims to indemnity. The books of Moses went into these issues as they touched, first, on ancient desert life, and, later, on the days before and after the exile. In Jesus' time a scribal tradition updated these decisions but we have no written record of it earlier than the Mishnah (ca.180 of the Common Era). In any event, the learned argued and decided how Jewish morality was to be lived in difficult cases. Jesus is reported as approving their activity ("Do everything and observe everything they tell you" [Matthew 23:3]). But this act of confidence in their decisions occurred once, whereas Jesus insisted constantly that his hearers had to decide for themselves which actions were conformed to covenantal fidelity and which were a breach of it.

"I have come to call sinners, not the just" (Mark 2:17), Jesus said. The call he issued was to the righteousness characteristic of the final age he inaugurated, not the pale copy of God's righteousness he was encountering. He taught that the Sabbath was at humanity's service, not the other way around (see Mark 2:27). This idea was later to be recorded as a rabbinic axiom and was probably of long standing. Being the best of Judaism, it is a Christian heritage, having become such as a saying of Jesus. Every written precept, he taught, even the most solemn ones that touch on the worship of God, yield to human need. This was not Jesus grudgingly allowing an exception. It was the heart of the rabbinic interpretation of divine teaching and he promulgated it in full force. He also taught: "In the measure you give you shall receive, and more besides" (Mark 4:24).

Jesus was a maximalist in moral theory, not a minimalist. His guiding precept was, "Do more." He knew the divine prodigality and taught it as the only human standard. "Be...perfect as your heavenly Father is perfect," he enjoined, meaning that his followers should give wholeheartedly, totally (Matthew 5:48).

How could anyone make it through life when such giving seemed beyond human capacity? This question had a single response: "Trust." Jesus was convinced that with faith or trust in God people could accomplish marvels of upright behavior.

The commandments of the decalogue ("the ten words") and the many others found in the Law were fully binding for Jesus, like those on the respect owed to parents by their adult children (Mark 7:10; see Exodus 21:17; Leviticus 20:9). A man who said he had kept the commandments from his youth (including the prohibition of defrauding fieldworkers [Leviticus 19:13]; see Jesus on the victimizing of widows by the pious [Mark 12:40]) was told to sell what he had and give the money realized to the poor

(Mark 10:21). Later tradition made a "counsel" of this passage but in context it looks like a command. Any who are rich and wish to be disciples have a hard time wriggling out of it. Jesus presumed that the precepts of the Torah would be kept. His interpretations never denied them but often led to inconvenient conclusions flowing from them. One cannot imagine him entertaining the question, "How little must I do to gain eternal life?" Jesus may have thought you could get rich and stay honest but we have no word of his on the subject (see Mark 10:23, 25, 27). He was equally hard on authoritarian behavior (Mark 10:42–44), which was compounded by making a holy show (Matthew 6:1–6, 16–18; Mark 12:38–39).

Is Catholic morality based on the assumption of a band of equals or a company of teachers telling others what to do? Jesus envisioned a company of equals at the level of behavior who would come after him. They would look for the rule of God and expect the cross. His disciples would be people like him who would give their lives for others (see John 15:13). Millions have accepted the invitation: parents living for children, grown children for parents, spouses for one another, exiled immigrant laborers for their families, soldiers dying for compatriots and even for strangers. They do not think of themselves as victims but as disciples of Christ.

Jesus taught that what was due to God should be rendered to God and what was due to the Caesar should be rendered to Caesar (Mark 12:17). He left all questioners since that time to work out which debt was which, implying strongly that God's demands on Jesus' fellow Jews came first. As Christians go higher in the service of either God or Caesar, they seem to find the distinction harder to make. First of all the commandments is the love of God. The love of neighbor is second. So Jesus taught in his summing up of the Torah (Mark 12:28–33). This linking of two biblical precepts (Deuteronomy 6:5 and Leviticus 19:18) was probably a rabbinic convention in Jesus' day. We know it became such later. It gained currency in the gentile world through Christianity, circulating as Jesus' "twofold law of love." It rang the death knell of long-standing grudge and revenge as allowable forms of Christian behavior. The corpse is slow in being buried.

Some have asked whether Jesus was realistic in what he looked for. Did his moral program befit a messianic age that was always on the brink of arriving, more than a world that hobbled on for millennia? The four gospels show that the early Christian communities, with all their apocalyptic hope, acted as though the world they knew would be around for a while. From the start they tried to live out these moral precepts of his in the only world there was. The six famous "antitheses" of the Sermon on the Mount are a case in point (Matthew 5:21–48). Jesus teaches, "But I say to you...," and Christian scholars argue about how much in each of these teachings is proper to the last age in its fullness and how much is achievable in the present. They are given to reckoning which of the six precepts Jesus interpreted radically but did not change, which he abrogated, and which they cannot be sure of. Rabbinic scholars seem to recognize immediately the activity Matthew has Jesus engaging in. It is not a case of text versus text to resolve the apparent contradiction, least of all of Jesus changing the Law. It is an exploration of the utmost demand of God that the commandment might contain. The formula was evidently a familiar rabbinic one which did not in any way pit the expositor's view against Torah.

The six conclusions of these juxtapositions of Matthew 5:21–48 are well known. On the principle of inner intention (*kavanah* in Hebrew), Christians are committed by their great teacher to the following: abstaining from abusive speech and unreconciled anger; refraining from lustful thoughts; not dismissing their spouses; not needing to back up their word with an oath; not offering resistance to injury; and loving enemies even beyond the point of praying for them. The church received this teaching not as a set of ideals attainable only in the final age but as a set of demands it had to live by in the present. It was community behavior that could not but be noticed by outsiders, who then could only marvel and praise God for it (Matthew 5:14–16). John summed up this moral stance as the behavior of friends who had a single commandment from God: to love one another as their great friend Jesus had loved them (John 15:12, 17). The patent unrealism of such a demand was relieved by the promise of Jesus' loving action within them to achieve it, as of a vine giving sap and life to branches (John 15:4–8).

Is Gospel Morality Too Idealistic? Too Nonspecific?

The basic principle of Christian morality is mutual love within the community of believers. If it is genuine it cannot have an exclusive character. It will, of its nature, be diffusive even though only those who know the love of Christ will know how to respond to it fully. This means that the Catholic faith community within the wider Christian family, if it is faithful to Jesus' commandment, will be supportive, compassionate, forgiving, and loving to all within it and to any who bear the name of Christ. Respect and service to all outside that family of faith must follow. Like love and marriage, "you can't have one without the other."

Some outsiders say respectfully that self-giving love as the norm for human behavior has a touch of madness about it. With specific teaching on specific matters such as that provided in Tanak (the Jewish Scriptures) or the holy Qur 'an, they say, you know where you stand. Jew and Muslim, for all their differences, feel more at one with each other than either does with the Christian when it comes to questions of human conduct. Even the upright who are not religiously oriented welcome the thought-out ethical systems based on Plato or Confucius or Kant. They may not be specific but, within a broad framework, they are clear. Moral dilemmas always come at people in specific, not general, ways. They need specific guidance. The Hebrew Scriptures and the Qur 'an deal with cases. That is why non-Christians often look on Jesus' love command as not of sufficient help.

The second- and third-century churches met the difficulty by framing lists of precepts to live by, culling them chiefly from the gospels with a few from Paul and the pastoral epistles (1 and 2 Timothy, Titus). It was biblical morality understood in the stern but clement way of Jesus. What else could it be? Much later the lofty Stoic teaching of men like Seneca (not "stoic" in the popular bite-the-bullet sense) was put in the service of Christian morality. Later still the same happened to the Platonism that most of the church fathers were reared on. Both ethical traditions were employed in the systematizing of gospel teaching.

No one can fault these developments except those purists who think that any expression of Christian life which is not biblical is an adulteration. Some of the Reformers felt the need to oppose the medieval coupling by Aquinas of Aristotle's cardinal virtues with the theological virtues of faith, hope, and charity. This scheme provided seven headings under which every salutary act and sin—if they were habitual they were termed virtue and vice—could be placed. There was no great harm in it, any more than there is harm in trying to determine whether the human nature God has endowed us with provides clues as to the way we should act. It could even have done much good. The inherent danger, however, should be self-evident. The Christian moralist—and ordained preachers are by definition public moralists—can always risk trusting the philosophical conclusions of theologians more than the true "teacher come from God" (John 3:2). The Catholic especially, because of a long-standing espousal of the concept of natural law, is open to the charge of setting revealed knowledge aside and putting human knowledge in its place.

To be sure, neither the Jewish Scriptures nor Jesus nor his disciples had anything to say about making a profit from insider trading or having a vasectomy or lying on the witness stand to "preserve national security." Biblical precepts, however the Christian approaches them, must be applied to life situations. A few general questions must prevail. What does love demand in this case? How is the covenantal commitment made in baptism to God and the community sustained or damaged by this action? Has the image of Christ been enlarged or diminished, not to say destroyed, by some in the church to the spiritual ruin of those outside? Believers must make these determinations in every case, confident that the whole church is making them along with them.

The questions are not easy to answer. Jesus left it to God and his hearers to judge what was righteousness and what was sin in them. Only those most devoted to Christ and the gospel can guide others in resolving their consciences. These guides must be persons of learning. It must be evangelical learning, not merely human jurisprudence (which even a faithless person could administer justly). No one can tell others in the church when their act was sin because motivation is hidden from the eye. Lovers of God who are prudent—meaning sagacious, not timid—can describe actions that have the character of sin. Because they are prudent they never, in public or in private, declare anyone's actions but their own to *be* sins. They normally do not do much public denunciation because they are too busy laboring, teaching, and healing in ways calculated to eliminate the conditions of sin.

At times, though, like Jesus they must engage in public denunciation and then forthrightly: "You pay tithes on mint and herbs and seeds [contribute generously to church causes?] while neglecting the weightier matters of the law, justice and mercy and good faith" (Matthew 23:23). Unquestionably, teachers of the Christian way of life must speak out. They can only speak confidently, however, for or against that behavior on which there is wide consensus in the church. Otherwise they will be enunciating particular moral theologies—some of very recent vintage—and not the commitment of the whole church to gospel morality.

Although followers of Christ must show compassion toward weak or sinful behavior, they may not condone such behavior. Jesus never confused the sin with the sinner.

Some who are Catholics seek approval for their untraditional courses of action. When it is withheld they accuse fellow believers of hardness of heart, saying they feel alienated from the church that will not approve their behavior. Charity, for them, is letting everyone do what she or he wishes to without let or hindrance. But Jesus was intransigent on right and wrong. He was a "hard-liner" because the one he called his Father was. He forgave and taught forgiveness even to seven times seven times. Not once, however, did he acquiesce in a wrong way of acting.

The Morality of the Early Churches

For the greater good of the church at Corinth, St. Paul passed public sentence in Jesus' name on a man guilty of incest (1 Corinthians 5:3). The sentence was ejection from the community. Immoral believers are not to be associated with, he said (v. 9). Lawsuits taken outside the community are a scandal (6:1). "Why not put up with injustice, and let yourselves be cheated?" (v. 7), he asks. And he means it.

Paul's basic argument against Christian males' returning to their prostitutes, as they do while claiming to be "above the law," is that whoever is joined to the Lord is one flesh, becomes one spirit, with him (6:16–17). Commitment to the community and to its Lord makes such deviant conduct unthinkable. Paul knows nothing of the right to privacy in the brothel, or victimless crimes. Lest anyone think that his only concern is for the male offender because he is the one baptized, observe the value Paul puts on casual sex as something that involves two human beings as human. The woman may be a victim but, by the man's taking her, he treats her as only wives should be treated (he becomes "one body with her," "one flesh" [6:16]). A lifetime of tender concern is the sole fitting outcome of a "one-night stand"!

In any consideration of morality Paul looks first to the effect on the believing community, then to individuals only as they belong to that community. "We pray God that you [plural] may do no evil, not in order that we may appear approved but simply that you may do what is good.... Encourage one another. Live in harmony and peace" (2 Corinthians 13:7, 11). He uses lists of things that must always be done and may never be done, a convention of his time (see Romans 1:24–32; Galatians 5:19–23). He has the usual Jewish prejudice that pagans were in general an amoral lot, but that is not paramount in his teaching.

The basic reason Paul gives for why the familiar biblical morality must be adhered to is of first importance: "See that no one returns evil to any other; always seek one another's good and for that matter, the good of all" (1 Thessalonians 5:15). "My [fellow believers (adelphoi)], if someone is detected in sin, you who live by the spirit should gently set [that one] right, each of you trying to avoid falling into temptation.... Help carry one another's burdens; in that way you will fulfill the law of Christ" (Galatians 6:1–2). But hard-headed Paul, even if he believes in joint accountability, does not believe in joint guilt: "Each [one] should look to his [or her] own conduct....Everyone should bear his [or her] own responsibility" (Galatians 6:4, 5).

As we explore the demands of Christian morality in subsequent chapters, we shall see that, reductively, they come to carrying one another's burdens. Sin is living for the self alone. Virtue is living for the other. Catholic life is communitarian but it goes outside the household of faith. It is determined by the needs of the whole human community.

The "Epistle of James" looks like a letter but it is a collection of sayings. These moral maxims which circulated in an early Greek-speaking church purport to come from an apostle. Much in James is familiar moral teaching but it emerges, along with Revelation, as the apostolic excoriation of social evil most like the message of the prophets (see James 5:1–6; Revelation 18). The First Epistle of John spells out what "love for the world" means, the immorality that Christians seem to fall into most readily. Ephesians is a treatise that Paul did not write but that contains some of the most moving moral exhortation in the New Testament (see especially Ephesians 4:25–5:21).

The ethical teaching proposed in the second-century writings contains nothing we do not expect to find, beyond the formal prohibition of exposure of infants and abortion (Didachē 2.2).

Neither of the two wrongs is mentioned in the Bible, but then contraception—well known to the ancient world—is not to be found there either. Jewish tradition forbade all these practices and the preachers of the gospel concurred.

Extended reflection on states of mind and heart previous to wrongdoing did not surface in writing until St. Augustine of Hippo (396–430 C.E.). Moral theorizing, in the sense of providing reasons that certain acts are right and others wrong, and categorizing them, was not an activity of the first four Christian centuries. The church fathers knew that learned pagans did this, but they had a surer source: the teaching of God delivered through Moses and refined by Jesus.

Resort to moral theology, when it enters the Christian tradition, is not to be deplored. Such would be a fitting response to it only if the teaching of Jesus and the apostolic writers were mysteriously left out of account. Jesus in his own person, we repeat, is the morality of all Christians who live the life of the church.

3

Is There
a Natural Law?

Affectionate alumni of a U.S. seminary in foreign parts before
World War II (not one of the Roman colleges) used to tell priests
who had endured six stateside years in rigidly Tridentine seminaries that in their overseas college of a great university the rule
of the house until sundown was the decalogue; after that, natural law. Would such whimsical recollections have been possible
in Protestant churches, many of whose seminaries had as strict
rules as Catholic ones? The answer is no because the concept of
natural law was a fugitive in most Protestant seminary courses
on the subject of Christian ethics (although Luther retained it in
his 1525 treatise *Against the Heavenly Prophets* as underlying the
ten commandments).

Natural law within Protestant circles survived in some form
in required courses in moral philosophy offered in the eighteenth and nineteenth centuries at church-related colleges. That
meant almost all of them until the Morrill (land-grant college)
Act of 1862. Most often the president of an institution like

Harvard, Dartmouth, Yale, or Princeton would teach the moral philosophy course himself. The ethics taught would be largely Platonic-Stoic via Cicero and Seneca, interlaced with a modicum of Aristotle's *Ethics* and a good measure of Kant's moral imperative. (The latter stated that one should "act as if the maxim from which you act were to become...a universal law." Put another way, since rational nature exists as an end in itself, no rational creature should ever be used as a means but always as an end.)

Ever since a code that incorporated natural law was produced by the lawyers of the Byzantine emperor Justinian in 534, Catholics have held to the concept of a law of nature that is binding on all because they are human. This collection of laws stated, on the basis of the teachings of the church fathers, that the Roman *ius publicum* (people's law) and the gospel were at one in assuming that there is a binding law of nature. Both taught that humans always had to act as befitted their humanity, never otherwise.

The twelfth-century canonists, some of whom became popes, adopted this principle wholeheartedly. It was worked out theoretically by the prince of medieval theologians, Thomas Aquinas (1226?–74). He had Aristotle's *Ethics* available to him in Latin via an Arabic translation and saw in it an admirable basis for a philosophical discussion of human acts—namely, the free acts that all should or should not perform.

Aquinas conducted this discussion in the second part of his *Summary of Theology*. He dealt with morality as the correct human response to the God of all peoples, including those who believed in divine grace and providence. God had revealed laws to live by and held out to those acquainted with this revelation divine assistance to keep them. Aquinas thought that sin had not invalidated the essential principles of nature, therefore that even persons without a revelation from God could know how they ought to act. This was contrary to Augustine's pessimistic view of the damage sin had done to human nature and was challenged by the Reformers as Pelagian.

The Doctrine of Natural Law as Ultimately Biblical

Do the teachings of the Bible about human conduct which are primary for Christians claim that people can know by reason how they ought to act? Did the Jews and early Christians who wrote the books of the Bible think that there was a law written in the heart to which the precepts given through Moses and Jesus gave religious sanction? The answer to both of those questions is yes and no. Here is how things went.

The people of the Bible—Hebrews, later Israelites and then Jews—were not given to speculation. They did not write treatises on human nature (not having a word for *nature* or even for *human*, for that matter) or on what acts conformed and did not conform to it. Being nonspeculative, however, did not mean they were stupid.

The Scriptures this people wrote down and revered, even the parts earliest written, assumed that there were certain things the God of Israel would have them do and not do. This was because their God was holy, a word that means "separate" in Hebrew. In context in the Bible it always includes the notion of "righteous" or "ethical." Their rule of conduct as a people was what the Lord required of them. This was always identical with what was good for Israel. Their all-holy God was incapable of commanding them to do what was bad for them as a people.

You might think that a people whose morality was situated fundamentally in the will of the Lord would have fallen into the trap of supposing this God capricious—now willing one thing, now its opposite, to establish the power the Lord held over them. They never did. They could not imagine murder to be a good thing, or the death of their enemies a bad thing. Stealing from a fellow countryman (the word we translate "neighbor") was unthinkable. Pillaging the crops and possessions of other peoples was not only thinkable, it was a righteous act.

Does this sound like the morality of tribe or clan—words that nonanthropologists (like most of us) use interchangeably? It ought to, for so it was: a rigid ethic that bound the members of the people to act in one way with their own and quite otherwise with outsiders. It was thoroughly consistent. It admitted of no exceptions and very few mitigating circumstances.

Other examples of the moral code of this people included the following: A man could have plural wives or sex with numerous female slaves, but a woman could not have plural husbands or sex with anyone but her husband. Homosexual behavior and sex with animals were held in the same abhorrence as adultery. A woman who had sex before marriage (unless, of course, she had been raped) was severely dealt with; a man's "way with a maid" was regulated by a scale of repayments to the humiliated father or brother.

And so it went with infringements of property rights, lying, giving false witness, dealing lightly with "the Name," disrespecting aged parents. By the time all this behavior was codified in the five books of Moses—a codification that took place after the exile (586–37 B.C.E.)—much of the meaning of the ancient legislation about specific cases had been lost. It was the task of the proto-rabbis, beginning about 85 C.E. at Yavneh in Judea, to provide an updating of this legislation from antiquity to their own day. They wished to show Jews how they could observe even its most obscure precepts.

Where did this code morality of the Bible come from, so noble in its successive refinements over the ages down to Jesus' day? Tracking its major commandments and prohibitions through the codes of Israel's giant neighbors to the east, Assyria and Babylonia, one finds that the moral code of the Bible was simply part of the culture of the land between the rivers. Israel possessed its code as the patrimony of a people of the region. In adapting it, it gave every part it adopted a YHWH meaning. All that was prescribed was seen as the will of the all-holy God. What the Lord demanded was for the people's good. No questions were asked. The righteous behavior of the people fulfilled the terms of the covenant their God had made with them.

However the successive modifications of the common core of Middle Eastern morality were achieved, Israel's conduct became more clement than that of its neighbors while remaining rigorously just. Thus, the precept "...life for life, eye for eye, tooth for tooth, hand for hand, foot for foot, burn for burn, wound for wound, stripe for stripe" (Exodus 21:23–25) was a word of restraint in a culture not known for restraint. This biblical commandment did not demand the exaction of justice, as is widely understood. It said that true justice is different from unbridled reprisal. By Jesus' day the command was being fulfilled by settlements in money. Jesus took the mitigation even further, teaching that one should waive the rights one had in justice as a way of fulfilling the sublimest meaning of the precept (Matthew 5:39–42).

Did early Judaism (the period that started at Yavneh in the time of Joḥanan ben Zakkai, ca. 70) or early Christianity consolidate its moral teaching in such a way that either could be said to have a theory of morality? "Theory" in this usage means the rationale behind a system of laws or precepts binding rational creatures, the content of which is ascertainable by human reason. The answer is no in both cases. There was no such systematic rationale.

It is common to hear a view such as the following: "Jews and Christians not only affirm the existence of such a system [of morality], they also identify it with part of the code of conduct they take to be binding on themselves by virtue of religious truth."[1] But this expresses a development that was to come well after the apostolic age and much later among Jews. The Hebraic spirit was one of praise of God by keeping every divine commandment (see Psalm 119:6) and concentrating on the marvels of the Law (v. 18). This the Lord taught out of goodness and kindness (v. 68). The Bible contains practically no inquiry into what people could know about correct human conduct apart from the Law. Sporadic praise can be found in the Bible for the spirit that God has implanted within creatures to help them know the divine wisdom. This hardly counts as an inchoate theory of natural law. The same can be said for the isolated statement in Genesis 1:26 that the human creature is made in the image and likeness of God.

The late-written Wisdom of Solomon (first century B.C.E.), composed in good Greek by a Hellenized Jew, rails at the stupidity of those who have failed to recognize the Artificer after examining the works of creation. They mistake some of the works of creation for gods (13:1–9). Moral perversion of every sort is the necessary result of idolatry (14:23–26). In one place in the Book of Wisdom an interior reliance on reason is called a safeguard against superstition and fear (17:11–12), but this idea, which has no biblical history, is not further developed.

Saint Paul, again in only one place in the Bible, argues as Wisdom does when he accuses pagans of having exchanged the truth of God for a lie. As a result, he says, they have been abandoned to degrading passions (Romans 1:25–26). The pagans have not acknowledged God as they could have (1:19, 28) and God has left them to their "corrupt mind" to do wildly unbefitting things (1:28). But the pagans, who have never heard of Mosaic Law, are a law to themselves and can point to the substance of the law written in their hearts (2:14–15).

Saint Luke thinks it proper to put on Paul's lips in a speech before pagans the argument that as God's offspring, we are culpable if we suppose that deity can be represented by anything like an idol (Acts 17:22–31). He has Paul make no matching argument, however, that as rational creatures we should know how to behave morally. That approach to imperatives of conduct did not fall within the ordinary Jewish ken, nor for that reason within the early Christian ken.

How the Church Availed Itself of Natural Law Theory

It should be helpful here to trace the history of the doctrine of natural law and its entry into Christian moral discourse. It was the Stoics, not Plato or Aristotle, who formulated the first reasonably clear concept of morality. They held that the common rationality of all humans was the basis of the divine law. Aristotle did not get that far. He stopped short at defining ethical virtue as the virtue of the citizen of a good city, not of the person as a person. He did identify practical wisdom *(phrónēsis)* as the determinant of the "middle way" which constitutes virtue for the free citizen. But he did not strongly feature the connection between virtue and a law of reason. Stoicism did, as the following quotation from Cicero (Stoicism's purveyor to the Latin West) should indicate:

> True law is right reason in agreement with nature; it is of universal application, unchanging and everlasting; it summons to duty by its commands and averts from wrongdoing by its prohibitions.... It is a sin to try to alter this law, nor is it allowable to try to repeal any part of it, and it is impossible to abolish it entirely.... There will not be different laws at Rome or at Athens, or different laws now and in the future, but one eternal and unchangeable law will be valid for all nations and for all times, and there will be one master and one ruler, that is, God, over us all, for God is the author of this law, its promulgator and its enforcing judge. *(De Republica* III, xxii, 33)

This is the Stoic ideal of the universal law that befits the cosmopolis, or entire human family, rendered in more personally theistic terms. It passed into the *ius naturale* (law of nature) of the Roman jurists. The Christian writer Lactantius preserved Cicero's definition for the Catholic tradition. It went from him to Justinian, the Christian lawgiver. Close to this concept of natural law was the Stoic idea of human equality, again available in Cicero's expression of it:

> Those creatures who have received the gift of reason from nature have also received right reason, and therefore also the gift of law, which is right reason applied to command and prohibition. If they have received law they have received justice also. Now all have received reason; therefore all have received justice. *(De Legibus* I, x, 29; xii, 33)

There should be no difficulty in discerning how the early Christians trained in rhetoric (that is, philosophy, letters, and speech) discovered in writings such as these the law of the LORD praised by the Psalms and Christ's twofold law of love. They identified these pagans as forerunners of the gospel. Some even maintained that Seneca, a native of Spain and brother of Gallio, the proconsul of Achaia (see Acts 18:12–17), must have known Saint Paul in his lifetime, so noble was his Stoic concept of morality.

From the Philosophers to the Lawyers

The *Corpus Iuris Civilis* (the Justinian code) referred to in the third paragraph of this chapter was a product of far-reaching significance. A.P. Dentrèves, an Italian at Oxford, to whom this chapter is much indebted, does not hesitate to place it second after the Bible in influence on the history of the human race.[2] The chief question for us is: Were the jurists drawn upon by Emperor Justinian's lawyers philosophically oriented, in the manner of the Greek and Roman theorists of natural law?

The *Corpus* was in three parts: an educational handbook called the *Institutes*, a *Digest* of systematically arranged excerpts from earlier jurists, and a *Code* (i.e., codification) of imperial constitutions or decrees. This work came out of the East rather than the West. It was a mosaic rather than a project conceived in a unitary fashion.

The *Corpus* called law "a knowledge of divine and human things," "a theory of right and wrong" that has intrinsic worth, namely that of reason. It placed the jurist alongside the priest in his ministry of furthering what is good and equitable through the correlatives of law and justice. The law of nature corresponded to that which is always *bonum et aequum* (good and equitable). The word "always" may be a subsequent interpolation.

The answer to the question about the Byzantines' commitment to a *philosophical* theory of natural law varies, depending on which predecessors are cited. The *Digest* stated that an early third-century jurist named Ulpian, who was much quoted in the *Digest*, had written in a (now lost) book of *Institutes* that natural law is what nature has taught all animals, both humans and beasts alike, concerning mating, procreation, and the rearing of their young. Natural law is not the same as the "law of peoples," he said, which only humans have.

On the other hand an earlier jurist named Gaius, whose work entitled *Institutes* we possess (ca. 160 C.E.), bracketed the two (that is, natural law and the law of peoples). Ulpian's contemporary Paulus joined Gaius in seeing the universal validity of certain principles that are rational, accepted by all humanity, and inherently useful and good.

There emerged from the *Corpus* of Justinian a clear division between those like Ulpian, who saw nature as the inspiring motive for certain laws (thus, slavery could be declared against nature) and human convention as the motive for other laws (e.g., the foundation of kingdoms, the division of property), and those like Gaius, who thought that natural reason had led people equally to adopt the laws of morality and the laws of nations. From this brief summary it should be obvious that in the *Digest* there was no single, clear concept of natural law and the behavior it governed.

No one can be sure how these ambiguities entered into Justinian's work, whether because of development in theory over several centuries or because of the growth of a new conception of human life that would "find its full expression in Christianity."[3] Some say that numerous definitions of natural law which did not originate in the classical period were inserted by Byzantine hands.

Whatever the case, the *Digest* and the *Code* laid a claim to universal validity based on the nature of humanity. This was uppermost in the compilers' minds. Justinian affixed his own name to the following statement in the *Institutes*: "The laws of nature, which are most equally observed by all peoples, remain always stable and immutable, enacted as they are by some kind of divine providence" (I, ii, 11). In this body of laws, *natura hominis* tends to mean that which is humanly normal while *contra natu-ram* is the abnormal. A "natural possession" is at the root of all property. A "natural cognate condition" underlies matters of the family, biologically speaking. A "civil cognate condition" characterizes the political aspect of the human family. The jurists who wrote the *Corpus* were trying to find the rule that corresponds to the nature of things, that is, to a concrete situation of fact and life. They did not think they had in natural law a complete system of rules governing all cases. It was for them a means of interpretation, a way to initiate discussion of specific cases. Nowhere in the *Corpus* did they put natural law above divine positive law. Certainly the church has never done so because it knows that its primary charge is discovering and applying clearly "the law of Christ" (Galatians 3:6).

Natural Law's Entry into the Mainstream of Catholic Morality

If the notion of natural law had remained within the confines of philosophical speculation, even with the church's sanction, it would never have come to prevail. Embodied in the Byzantine-Roman imperial tradition, however, the theory of natural law exerted a widespread influence. The Roman system of laws was venerated as the expression of natural justice. Roman public law in the Eastern Empire could be hailed as universally valid because it coincided with the law of nature. But these propositions, which the learned accepted readily, were not enough to recommend it widely to the church's moral teachers.

In 1140 a monk of Bologna named Gratian compiled a body of extant church laws, the first in what later came to be known (in 1441 at the Council of Basel) as *Corpus Iuris Canonici*. This was intended to match Justinian's civil compilation. Gratian's work is generally called the *Decretum*, although he gave it the name *The Concord of Discordant Canons*.

The opening paragraph of the *Decretum* states: "Humanity is ruled by two laws: natural law and custom. Natural law is that which is contained in the Scriptures and the gospel." That statement could mean that the revelation made to Israel and culminating in Jesus Christ confirms and implements the conduct required of human nature. It could also mean that what can be discovered by analyzing human nature is contained in the Bible. In either case it is a portent of what was to come. For the appearance given, whatever the intention, was that gospel morality rests on a philosophical basis and its demands can be spelled out in a code of laws. Perhaps considerably less is being said, namely that canon law was simply serving as the principal vehicle of the doctrine of the divine law of nature, as contrasted with the human law of custom.

If the law of nature goes back to God as the biblical revelation does, the claim may merely be that there is no conflict. The only danger would lie in supposing that the law of nature makes the gospel needless, or that gospel morality is merely a confirmation of it. In such case the teachings of the gospel would be betrayed by a philosophical teaching meant to be its handmaid. The natural law of the medieval canonists was not simply, however, that of the Greco-Roman jurists and philosophers. It had been rendered Christian by the fathers of the church. The church fathers had come to identify natural law with the law given by God to Adam, a general and primitive law of the human race. Christian writers like Saint Ambrose and Saint Augustine had developed the idea of a "natural law written in the heart" on the basis of Romans 2:15 and of an innate capacity to attain to the knowledge of this law. It was immutable, as Justinian said, because it was providential. The whole patristic tradition led up to Gratian's claim of the embodiment of the law of nature in the Scriptures.

The medievals took the case a step further than the church fathers by maintaining that the evidence of reason and that of revelation were correlative. They held that the folly of the cross did not flatly contradict worldly wisdom but could be reconciled with it. In a new spirit of optimism that was quite different from Augustine's pessimistic setting of the Earthly City against the

Heavenly, the world and the kingdom were held to have much to say to each other. Reason and faith were not incompatible. Nature was not depraved but deprived, and the grace of redemption had rectified its deprived condition. The law of nature was no longer viewed as a lost ideal in virtue of humanity's fall but as a retrievable, rational basis for the morality of social institutions.

An entirely new view of human perfectibility thus began to succeed the Augustinian pessimism. It had as its goal the possibility of a Christian civilization. A system of natural ethics with the law of nature as its cornerstone began to be thought of as contributing to a thorough Christianization of human life.

Saint Thomas Aquinas was the most authoritative voice for what in the West came to be, after much struggle, the Catholic view of moral life. He could not have held the ethical doctrine he did but for his view of God and the universe, and the place of humanity in it:

Supposing the world to be governed by divine providence...it is clear that the whole community of the universe is governed by the divine reason. This rational guidance of created things on the part of God...we can call the eternal law....It [should be] clear that all things participate to some degree in the eternal law, insofar as they derive from it certain inclinations toward those actions and aims which are proper to them. But, of all others, rational creatures are subject to divine providence in a very special way, being themselves made participators in providence itself in that they control their own actions and the actions of others. So they have a certain share in the divine reason itself, deriving from it a natural inclination to such actions and ends as are fitting. This participation in eternal law by rational creatures is called the natural law.... It is as though the light of natural reason, by which we discern good from evil, and which is the natural law, were nothing else than the divine light in us. (*Summary of Theology*, Ia IIae, q. 91, art. 1 and 2)

Absolutely basic to St. Thomas's understanding was the light of reason, which was probably a rationalized version of the illumination doctrine Augustine derived from Plato. The capacity to think rationally gave the human creature a dignity and power that made it unique, both subject to God and cooperator with God.

The first and general precept of Aquinas's view of natural law is that good must always be done and evil avoided. Other, more specific precepts flow from that one. The first of these touches on all that makes for the preservation and transmission of human life. After that comes the inclination to know the truth about God and then to live in society (see *ibid.*, q. 94, art. 2).

Saint Thomas points out that as problems of human conduct grow more specific and complex, it becomes harder to know what the law of nature requires. He says that all humanly enacted laws are in accord with reason to the extent that they derive from the natural law. If a human law is at variance in any particular with the natural law, it is no longer legal but rather a corruption of law (*ibid.*, Ia IIae, q. 95, art. 2). This means in practice that allegiance to the state or, one assumes, to authorities in the church and family, can only be conditional. All can make unreasonable demands. Unjust laws (commands) are not properly laws. "They do not, in consequence, oblige in conscience."

Aquinas, being a Christian, had a lively awareness of sin and its consequences. He did not have a utopian view of human nature, as if human beings did not constantly have to pay the penalty of sin. But he says expressly that sin has not "invalidated the essential principles of nature," meaning that our sinful race can know the dictates of natural reason even though it may be impaired in fulfilling them. Purely natural—that is, rational— values remain available to all. People's conduct, both as members of social, religious, and political institutions and as individuals, must be judged in this sphere. Because of his basic conviction that "grace does not abolish nature but perfects it," Aquinas proceeds to a discussion of corporate and individual morality on the premise that a wounded but not corrupted nature has guidance available to it through reason and not revelation only. Moral judgments can be clouded, he acknowledges, by ignorance and a misdirected will or love arising out of sin or self-centeredness. Despite that handicap, natural law judgments can still be made.

Dealing first with Christian behavior under the aspect of the exercise of the virtues of faith, hope, and love, Aquinas discusses all three both in their fullness and in the possible sins against them. Here he is in the realm of what only revelation can disclose and the grace of Christ can achieve. In accord with the gospel he says that love is the only virtue that cannot be sinned against by excess.

Turning to the four Aristotelian cardinal virtues, hinges (cardines) on which swing most moral challenges and dilemmas, Aquinas searches for the mean between the extremes of excess and defect in exercising wise judgment (prudence), justice, moderation (temperance), and courage (fortitude). Aquinas categorizes moral choices all but exhaustively under these headings. He describes good and bad acts which, if persisted in, will lead to the habits of virtue or vice. Throughout he maintains that practical wisdom can determine whether or not a given choice accords with a rationally determined mean or middle ground. He does not at any point deny the additional motive to goodness provided by faith in Christ, or by the grace available to humans to help them know and do what is right.

D'Entrèves points out that "despite the stress which is laid upon the absolute and immutable character of natural law, the notion of it seems to be curiously flexible and adaptable."[4] Thus, positive laws are not to be expected to be based on natural law as on a rigid pattern. The human lawgiver has considerable freedom in interpreting and applying its general precepts. Catholic moralists have not always taken their cue from this caution of Aquinas. They have sometimes spelled out ethical demands on believers in the areas of family life and the use of speech and the offices of religion (less often, accountability and justice in society) as if human nature were an open book withholding no secrets. The natural law has sometimes wrongly been proposed as indicating how people must choose in facing quite specific moral dilemmas. Perhaps the most familiar cases today are in the areas of sexuality and medicine or surgery. There, a certitude is assumed concerning the natural law that can only be provided by long and deep reflection on the implications of the teachings of Jesus and the apostolic age.

The community known as church is called to be the moral teacher of its own members in the spirit of Jesus. Following this, those outside may take guidance if they wish. The church does well to say what all humanity is held to, believers and unbelievers alike, but here it is on less sure ground. There is a wide variety of peoples on the earth. There is also a mutability of human nature as the race comes upon new awarenesses or falls back on earlier barbarisms. These considerations are often not taken into account by churchmen of the West who assume that all humanity is both fixed and made in the Western cultural image and likeness.

Saint Thomas says that human nature can change by "addition," as when new institutions become necessary in view of the development of human activities. It can change by "subtraction," when "something ceases to pertain to the natural law which was formerly part of it." This means that for him natural law is a form of historical thinking, something that both its detractors and overzealous proponents deny to it. Asserting absolute and immutable values does not deny evolution and development. With the passage of time we *do* learn some things about our nature and its demands on us. The equal liberty of all people, and all peoples, which means an end to all slavery including the economic type, has been a long time dawning in Christian consciousness. The same is true of the full human freedom of women. Nothing in the nature of things allows for the domination of women by men, whether within marriage or outside it. The modification of human life through disease control, population control, and the conservation of resources is part of an ongoing discovery of what natural law does and does not require.

Most important of all, perhaps, is that the universal conviction of the past that war is an allowable human activity is yielding with glacial slowness to the awareness that nothing in the law of nature allows war.

Natural Law: A John the Baptist Deferring to Jesus

The limitations of natural law are as important to Catholic morality as is its scope. Like anything humanly deduced about the divine, there is the possibility of error as well as truth, abuse as well as use. Besides natural law, people have a conviction within and without the world's religious traditions that carefully conceived laws promulgated for the common good are not simply a check on criminality. They are a guide to public morality. Human laws restrain the wicked from wrongdoing by force and by fear, but they also direct the good in leading productive lives. God revealed the laws of Sinai and the gospel in order to lead humanity to its destiny. Revelation makes up for the shortcomings of human judgment and leaves no virtue unrewarded, no evil unpunished at the final judgment.

These three kinds of law—natural, human positive, and divine positive—are united in a complete and coherent system. The totality is known in its fullness to God alone, but the human race can glean some measure of its splendor and perfection and can live by it.

For Aquinas and those who understand him well, the natural order is the condition and the means of attaining a higher order. Nature does not abolish grace any more than grace abolishes nature. Reason and faith are closely allied, even the reason of sinful humanity. But faith is always the mistress and reason the handmaid. The order may not be reversed. Natural law can never replace the revealed order of Christian conduct nor supply for the "deficiencies" of faith's teaching. This being so—and all Catholic moral teachers maintain it in theory—it is a wonder that the ethical teachings of the Law and the prophets and of Jesus and the apostolic church have not long ago had a coherent, systematic deduction drawn from them: a biblical theology of Christian morality. When it is done it will not be primarily philosophical in orientation but evangelical. It will at the same time be both intelligent and intelligible.

Increasingly in the modern period Catholic teachers of morality ask those learned in the Bible for a theology of morals derived primarily from that source. The moral theologians say they are incapable of constructing it, yet they know that it is a need of the church. They are as aware as anyone that the documents of faith, the Scriptures, are the charter of Christian conduct. A theory of human nature that looks occasionally and not too anxiously for biblical warrant cannot be the way of life in Jesus Christ. In the present uneasy situation, numerous demands are placed on the consciences of Catholics. The correct responses to some of these demands are incapable of proof in the strict sense on natural law grounds. Yet it is maintained that the sources of revelation require those correct responses.

A moral tradition of relatively long standing deriving from biblical sources—the normal way Catholics know how they must act—does not exist to help solve many modern dilemmas. In this biblical morality, the variety within human nature through uneven development must be taken into account. A believing community, conscious of how Jesus its Lord would have it act in the service of God, must make these determinations on these grounds.

The Catholic morality appropriate for our times is slow in coming. It must be developed from the standpoint of what is clearly revealed and not from a rational process that is too readily equated with revelation. Reason will never lose its force in shedding light on the moral teaching of the Bible. The clearer beacon, however, is the teaching of Israel's prophets and sages and Jesus, the church's Lord. "He must increase," all overconfident natural law theories should cry out, "and I must decrease."

Jesus offered some very specific teaching about human conduct before God. All of it was a reiteration or refinement of what was found in his people's Scriptures. It was a very personal

morality—dealing with the relationships between the person
and society, among persons, and between the person and a personal God. Intention was primary for Jesus. He may have had in
mind the "objective quality of the act" but he never expressed it
that way, probably because his Semitic listeners would not have
understood the language. Jesus' teaching was practical and immediate, even casuistic. In numerous parables he placed before
his hearers cases in conscience ending with the question, often
implied, "How would you judge it?" From the motivations to
act that he proposed, from his constant assumption of freedom
to act, from his unequivocal commitment to human life and to
liberty and justice within that life, a quite thorough set of principles and practical applications can be deduced.

The Pauline epistles, whether authentic or written by another
hand, and the epistles of Peter and James and John, James especially, are a treasure house of specific moral proposals. Behind
them lie the explicit or implicit teachings of the Torah or Israel's
prophets.

The biblical theology of morals that the church so badly needs
has a rich lode to mine in the Scriptures. Ready at hand is the
tradition of the church in ethical matters. This is dependable
when it is time-tested but uncertain when it is not. Also standing by are fifteen centuries of acquaintance with and use of the
concept of natural law. They are a shining and burning light like
John, but not itself the true light. That light is Christ.

4

What to Do
About Possessions

In the first three chapters we have been exploring Catholic morality, intending to see whether there is anything distinctive about it or whether it can be called identical at all points with other Christian moralities. All Christian morality shares in general in the characteristics of the morality of first-century Judaism from which the church came to birth. This is largely a code of conduct incumbent on all humans. God's self-revelation, however, delivered first through Moses and later through Christ and the church, made it more specific and proposed divine assistance for its fulfillment.

I have proceeded until now on a few self-evident assumptions from the New Testament, holding in abeyance the differences, if any, that the divisions among Christians mean for the conduct of a life lived in Christ. Catholic, Orthodox, and Protestant moralities assume in common the reality of the Holy Spirit as the interior teacher who both illumines and gives the power to fulfill the law of Christ. An important Catholic-Protestant difference of the last hundred years or so is that the church has increasingly for Catholics and decreasingly for Protestants served as the interpreter of what the law of Christ demands. The Protestant principle always allowed individual self-determination in matters of conscience. Liberal Protestantism has seen almost an abdication of the churches' function as moral teachers in personal affairs, even as this function grew in social matters. Conservative evangelical or fundamentalist morality, on the other hand, has assembled an arsenal of biblical texts as justifications for what the Christian may or may not, must or must not do. In general this morality is hearteningly rigorous as to person if not society. There are at the same time some alarming exegetical exercises in the search for biblical teaching on matters where the Bible is silent.

Having said so much, I now proceed further into the heartland of Catholic morality.

The Root of All Evils and Some Tangled Branches

The perception is widespread that, for Christianity, sexual deviance is immorality and morality is the use of sex exclusively within marriage. Such an identification is hardly the case. The central problem for the morality of the gospel, and hence for Catholic morality, is the sin of pride or rebellion against God. It takes the form of a claim of autonomy: complete self-determination. Often the code word "the church" is substituted for God. The clearest practical symbol of being free from all authority or control is money and what it can buy. The hatred and anger and lust fomented by greed are immediate corollaries. The observations that follow should make that clear.

The instability of marriage and family life in Western cultures in the last few centuries, especially the current one, has given the impression that sex, not greed, is the central problem of Christian morality. Sexual gratification expresses the tendency to acquisitiveness or greed, to be sure, but the love of money continues when all passion is spent and anything else that might have resembled love is dead. The fact that Jesus returned to the primordial biblical teaching on marriage has added to the above-named impression. In this teaching and in all the other "antitheses" of the Sermon on the Mount ("but I say to you" sayings; see Matthew 5:21–48), Jesus gives a rabbinic refinement of six cases—murder, adultery, the dismissal of wives by husbands, false swearing, restraint in retaliation, and love of neighbor—which are specifications or narrower focusings of biblical morality, but which in no instances are true antitheses.

Deductions About Modern Problems
The chief reason alleged for why the biblical moralities of both the Christian Scriptures and the Hebrew Bible are inadequate to the conduct of modern Catholic life is that these moralities do not take into account certain major problems of our time. Among these are participation in modern war, international corporate life, reproductive control by abortion, sterilization and contraception, the economic oppression of large populations by concentrated wealth, excessive nationalism, persecution for religious reasons, and sexism.

It is quite clear that specific moral teachings on the above questions must be deduced from the general principles and specific cases handed down by Moses, the prophets and sages, Jesus and postbiblical Jewish teachers like him, and the apostolic company that spoke in Jesus' name. For Christians, the fathers of the church did some of this deduction. So did the medieval schoolmen and the theologians of the Renaissance-Reformation and modern periods.

An Uneven Development
The development of specific moral teachings has proceeded on an uneven front. There can be no doubt of that. Some questions have received much attention, others little. Personal morality has been addressed far more than social, in good part because of

the way the confession of sins has been practiced in the Catholic West. There has been a "soft line" on violence, even in marriage, and a "hard line" on sexual sin; a neutral, not to say favorable, view of armed conflicts and a suspicion of activism for peace; a silence, if not disregard, with respect to the diversion of public moneys by persons with a public trust and a hard look at the theft of even small amounts in personal dealings.

The list could go on: scandal taken at individual marital infidelities but none at complicity in the prostitution industry; concern over the drug trade but none over the liquor trade; deep censure of fraud in business but little of the gambling, including church-sponsored gambling, that destroys lives and marriages; a centuries-long toleration of slavery which has a lively residue in racism; and the favoring in word and deed of the propertied classes.

It cannot be held that nothing may be taught by the church until everything is taught, or until all is taught with the same intensity. It can be held that a church of selective morality, whether the promulgators be lay or clerical or the two in concert, is an unworthy teacher in Christ's name. A serious problem is that when certain segments of the population resist a traditional understanding—for example, the supposition that men have a natural dominion over women—they are likely in the short run to receive church censure, even if in the powerful form of active disregard. When, on the other hand, women maintain that their marriages to psychotic or alcoholic or sadistically cruel men are not sacramental unions in Christ, they are likely to be told in one century that nothing can be done about it and in another to be cooperated with in the annulment process, or be given different responses in different countries or adjacent dioceses.

Change Acknowledged in Retrospect

The examples above are a way of saying by illustration that culturally stable views of human relations and evolving views are equally influential on Catholic morality. Sometimes the influences have good outcomes, sometimes bad. It is only after the passage of a century or two and much suffering that change is acknowledged in retrospect as having taken place. Often there is the bland assumption that there was no change. Such instances provide a powerful lesson that gospel morality and church law or practice do not always coincide.

For the people who live through that time, however—for example, the black Catholics unjustly discriminated against in their own church even now—there is little relief afforded from basically immoral settlements. Catholics in the various "states of life" have a handy solution for others about how much of the cross those others must carry. They sometimes confuse the saving wood of Calvary with the heavy and insupportable burdens that Jesus wrathfully said some religious teachers place on others.

In September 1987, on the occasion of the visit of Pope John Paul II to San Antonio, Texas, the Reverend Thomas Harvey, the executive director of Catholic Charities U.S.A., a social service organization that has 633 member agencies, shared an insight into Catholic morality with the pope in a brief public talk. He first mentioned that 34 million people in the United States, including one-quarter of the country's children, live in poverty. In his plea for some flexibility in looking for solutions to contemporary ethical dilemmas, Harvey said:

> Where people are suffering from such debilitating problems as divorce, diseases such as AIDS and the ambiguity of changing lifestyles, we ask patience of the church's teachings so that we do not close the door to opportunities for better solutions to these pressures of our changing world than our present wisdom easily affords.[1]

"Our present wisdom" is gentle code-language for unyielding certitude about morally ambiguous situations. Harvey was enunciating an old principle. *The Teaching of the Twelve Apostles* (75–125 C.E.) put it this way: "If you can bear the Lord's full yoke, you will be perfect. But if you cannot, then do what you can."[2] We seem to have lost the courage to say that. Catholic moral teaching has in various ages departed from its own deepest wisdom, counseling compassion for those who suffer as a result of its teachings when the relief needed was from the rigor of certain teachings themselves. Overzealous deduction from the teachings of Jesus and the apostles has caused much needless suffering over the Catholic centuries.

Jesus' Teaching: The Folly of Piling Up Riches

What follows is an exploration of the one matter Jesus was extremely rigorous about. If he taught any exceptions or flexibility in this matter, they are not recorded. Jesus took it as axiomatic that an excess of possessions could corrode the human soul. He never said how much ownership was too much. "You cleanse the outside of cup and dish, but within you are filled with rapaciousness and evil.... But if you give what you have as alms, all will be wiped clean for you" (Luke 11:39, 41).

There is no indication that rich people turned out in any numbers to hear Jesus' teachings. The gospels note the exceptions (Luke 8:3; John 19:38–39). The dispropertied, the landless poor, did. It was *they* whom Jesus warned constantly about what an attachment to possessions could do. In one of his stories, Jesus has God address as a "fool" the man who tore down his storage bins to build bigger ones (Luke 12:20).

Jesus told no tales that reproached his listeners for hoarding or miserliness (although there *was* a passing reference to moths and rust [Matthew 6:19]). Instead, he told stories about the folly of piling up wealth while supposing that it will lead to happiness. "Avoid greed in all its forms," he taught. "A person may be wealthy, but his possessions do not guarantee him life" (Luke 12:15). He was very severe on the rich, never saying a kind word for them. He knew that the rich are wise in their own eyes (Proverbs 28:11) and prone to apostasy and idolatry (Amos 3:4–14; Isaiah 2:6–8), violence and oppression (Job 20:19; Sirach 13:4–7). He spoke of them in no other way.

How Wealth Is Acquired

In those days there were only two ways to get rich honestly: to be born to a fortune or to marry one. Holding on to one's wealth was almost sure to require the same injustice as characterized the father or the spouse who amassed the fortune in the first place. Productive capital did not exist in Jesus' time. Its precedent was plunder, chiefly of the agrarian poor. It can well be asked whether there is such a thing in our time as productive capital without the rape of the poor somewhere in the world. Yet the phenomenon of money making money is not the problem. Money making money so that a person can spend $105 on dinner for two while people forage in garbage cans outside is the problem. Dinner for *one* at $105 is achievable only by robbing the people who are at the garbage cans.

Many young people in the United States harbor the dream of making a million dollars by the time they are thirty-five—some on the stock market or in corporate raiding, some in drugs, three or four by honest labor.

But no one can make millions within a few years by honest labor, only by favorable "deals." Those who do make a fortune by honest labor do not actually *earn* it. They realize these huge profits, and live with the belief that they have earned them (or earned their huge salaries), but it is a myth. No executive officers of companies earn their annual stipends unless twelve-hour days (which many people put in at $3.35 an hour) or ulcerated stomachs count as "earning." They are awarded them, or award them to themselves, in a system where compensation is far out of proportion to worth. Years of frantic air travel and hours on the telephone may have gone into the process of building a fortune, but the phrase "earning a salary around the million mark" is meaningless. The system that awards such salaries is dishonest because the money came from exploitation. This truism is illustrated in a thousand ways: electronics workers going blind in the Philippines wiring computers, seasonal workers the world over with no guarantees and no benefits (in Mexico, to bring low-priced fresh fruit and vegetables to the North American table), retired couples who did not read the fine print that said, "This may be a high-risk security."

Setting standards against participating in exploitation in today's economy could mean that no honest Christian could take a job, or at least most jobs, after high school or college. The first cry to be heard in response to descriptions of an exploitative economy is that "the system is too big and no one can buck it." Less pragmatically and under the banner of idealism, it is asked, "How are things ever going to get better if nobody tries to bring decency into the marketplace?"

A First Step

The fact is that consumer advocates, motivated by an ethical concern that is often nonreligious, devote their energies unreservedly to what is actually the Christian (and Jewish and Muslim) ideal of justice. Absolute fairness to the buyer is their stated goal. These advocates often allow themselves only modest salaries and lifestyle as a first step toward halting the oppression of ordinary people by unscrupulous vendors or industries too big to care.

Those who profess to follow Christ may not allow admission into their lives of greed in any form. In resisting greed in themselves, they take the first step toward justice for others. They refuse to amass more goods or property or money than they need (more accurately, than they foresee the reasonable need for).

Resisting greed is not a matter of forgoing earned income, least of all when one's family needs it or when a certain income level prevails in the segment of society in which one finds oneself. It is a matter of not defining oneself by what one has. The only worth that Jesus taught anyone to strive for was the worth of what one is. He was opposed to letting what one owned or clung to, reputation or image as much as possessions, define one's importance. He would not let things win the mastery over persons.

The Meaning of "Sell All You Have"

Sometimes people charge that, by demanding detachment from goods and money, Jesus had not only a rigorous ascetical ideal but also an unrealistic one. Close examination of his teaching shows that living a life of absolute justice fulfills the demands Jesus made of most people. Of the few who were able to do it, he required that they sell their possessions and give to the poor, then become disciples of him (see Luke 18:22). Most people on the earth—including many in this country—never acquire such a surplus that the commandment applies to them.

The gospels and the epistles indicate that even in the apostolic age there was no such thing as a totally dispropertied church. The Book of Acts describes a scheme of common ownership and support in an idyllic early Jerusalem. Elsewhere, however, we read of the great majority of believers who lived ordinary lives in cities and towns, as contrasted with the much smaller number who took literally Jesus' words to the rich young man. The latter have flourished ever since the days of the early church, often assisted in lives of poverty by stable income-earners in everyday circumstances. To become voluntarily poor you first need to have reached a certain level of possessions.

At various times, sects have arisen maintaining that unless one becomes poor by choice, as the rich young man was counseled to do, one cannot be a Christian. Thus, the followers of Wycliff or the "spiritual" Franciscans denied the title "Christian" to anyone who retained any ownership. The church has always censured sects that censure everyone's way of life but their own. But the church was indebted to them, even in their error, for reminding it of what the greater number always forget (or wish to suppress)—namely, that unless one holds possessions in a measure of contempt, one will forget the worth of the human spirit. In that sense, Jesus taught the most rigorous asceticism imaginable. His message was that whether your possessions be mean and few or rich and many you must control their distribution and use. You may not let them control you.

The Basic Asceticism: Absolute Justice

The question frequently asked by Catholics in an economy that works well for two-thirds of its people (obscenely well for the top bracket) and badly for one-third is, "Why can I not have everything that comes my way honestly and be a good Catholic, too?" Many do not ask the question. They assume that there is no question.

From all we know of Jesus' teaching, he would have first asked whether the person's money and possessions had come honestly or not. He told stories to make his profound moral points using the economy of his day, an economy built on taxing ordinary householders beyond endurance. The ownership class was expropriating the peasants' land after first having driven them into debt after crop failure. The situation is almost perfectly replicated in many Latin American countries and the Philippines, abetted by U.S. capital. Jesus would be just as able to direct his parables of theft at our economy.

"Once there was a certain executive officer who..." You can take it from there—the expense account game, large payments in cash going totally unrecorded for IRS purposes, substantial gifts accepted for no more meritorious reason than that one works for the "chief" (the chief of what does not matter) or for some embezzler highly placed. Jesus' parables on these matters would have been quite chilling, we may be sure.

Above, it was said that the basic asceticism Jesus laid on all was absolute justice. Talking about it is much easier than practicing it. How does one conduct oneself with total justice? Paying for everything you get is a good way to start. Not taking an unearned nickel from any person, any business, any municipal corporation, no matter how sloppy the accounting system, is another good way. If the money is not yours, put it back. Do not console yourself that some other stiff will only get it. Just be sure you are the stiff who passed it up. It is not yours.

If every Catholic in the land were to stop accepting every penny of unearned income tomorrow (and we are only 20 percent of the population), the shape of white-collar, blue-collar, and no-collar America would be vastly different. If every American were to succumb to this madness the banks would close, the market go amok, and the loading docks and highway freight come to a complete halt.

A Stark Principle

Classic Catholic moralists had a stark principle that could well be painted on signs planted on suburban church lawns, signs that now say things like "Free Soviet Jews." The principle is this: "An object cries out to its owner"; for the traditionalists who bemoan the passing of Latin: *"Res clamat ad dominum."* Maybe the parish council would want to claim the sentiment. Perhaps the pastor. The axiom is as old as the gospel, as old as the Law of Moses. It does not matter that the rightful owner is not always easy to identify, or that one puts oneself at risk in acknowledging one has committed a theft ("diversion of funds" we call it nowadays), or that one may by now be so deep in debt that any possibility of repayment is out of the question. The moralists' principle remains. The diverted money—whether $138 or $138,000—keeps shouting: "The taxpayers of the state own me"; "The shareholders in the corporation are my rightful owners"; "I am Stanislaus Zalewski's money, the boss's and no one else's."

Going public over one's deed of theft is not required. So goes the classic moral teaching. Giving to an anonymous charity will do if self-disclosure would mean the end of earning power or reputation. Token repayment will satisfy in the short run— anything to serve as a reminder that one owes the whole sum and will keep owing it until the last penny is returned, if that is humanly possible.

Some kind of compensation is always required. The Catholic penitential system has never permitted confession of an injustice to God alone while the victim goes uncompensated. The restoration of the stolen money or property is more important than confessing the theft to God. It is the one real proof of contrition before God. Saying one is sorry for injustice while doing nothing to rectify it has never been acceptable Catholic penitential practice. Such confessions of sin have always been considered invalid if there never was the intention to make restitution. "An object cries out to its owner."

Ambiguities in How Justice Must Be Done

The major problem for people who know that justice must be done is the ambiguity in modern life over *how* justice can be done. It is not always easy to know. If the dilemma about justice in today's world were simply a question of whether one can reuse uncancelled stamps or use the coins found in a pay telephone (there are plenty of the latter—all of North America is in a chronic state of overpayment!), life would be easier.

The genuine dilemmas over justice come at us in much more complex ways. "A day's work for a day's pay" is a good beginning. Fair enough. But say you find out that at the place where you work there is a well thought out scheme in place that benefits many in the company but that is also illegal and immoral. "A day's work for more than a day's pay" is the axiom that dominates. In that setting, what obligation does one have to be a whistle-blower, a reporter of the massive injustices perpetrated by others? The matter is complex because exposing the scheme would likely result in being fired and in hardship for one's family and oneself. "And how have you liked working here?"

How, in other words, do you cope with a deeply entrenched arrangement like kickbacks, double billing, or the agent's cut when rocking the boat would mean instant dismissal—worse, perhaps, violence to oneself or one's family? There is a poster in the subways of Philadelphia which says: "For Better Government, Report: Waste. Fraud. Abuse." A telephone number to the mayor's office is provided. Who dares to act on this moral imperative? Who has the time and the income to see it through? The principles are straightforward enough. Practicing them is the rub.

You stop cooperating with evil systems as soon as you discover a way to do so. Such a way may not present itself. *Any* attempt to opt out, even quietly, may put your job or your person at risk. That, you can perhaps endure. But your family? The principle of enduring the lesser of two evils operates here. Can one do anything to rectify the entrenched injustice? Often not. Usually not. Can one find a way not to be an active cooperator in the evil? Sometimes. Not always. In cases where it is impossible not to cooperate, you need to ask if you can find work elsewhere. Is other work available even if the income level is lower—in which case, could you live on it and support your family decently? Active participation in a dishonest scheme must stop immediately. Getting free of being a passive participant may take some time. Be assured that you are not the first person, nor will you be the last, to pay the high price of honesty.

Trying to Get Out of Unjust Systems

Sometimes there is no place to turn: the system you are trapped in at work is riddled with corruption and there seems to be no way out. The evil may be endured if the alternative is a greater evil to oneself and one's family. It must be remembered, though, how many upright Christians and Jews have anguished and planned and watched for their opportunity to pull out of companies, situations, even whole trades and professions, because they feared the loss of their souls—or their honor, it is much the same—if they stayed.

Needless to say, people prefer less anguished resolutions. A television program like "The People's Court" is popular because it shows justice being dispensed at high speed in relatively easy cases before the viewer's eyes—often on the seamiest moral basis. The program "60 Minutes" is even more popular for a different reason. Crooks and cheats squirm under the relentless questioning of the interviewers. If the crooks haven't "got theirs" yet you know they will shortly because of this national spotlight trained upon them. Often the courts or the district attorneys are watching on a Sunday night and the wheels of justice begin to turn Monday morning. Among the millions of viewers, though, there are the silent watchers who mean to keep their scams going undisturbed as usual on Monday morning. They think that their game isn't quite like any of the three they saw being skewered. And many viewers with troubled consciences cannot think of a way out of the boxes they are in.

The Struggle to Do Justice to All

Personal honesty and the maintenance of a modest standard of personal possessions are easy matters to face relative to the demands on the Catholic conscience created by a social order not of one's making. Living at peace with one's conscience in the midst of nationwide or global injustice makes individual believers wonder how they can seek liberty and justice for all. As a formula of words it is easy. Advancing it as a social reality is hard. Here are some specific problems.

Capitalist and Socialist Systems The capitalist system is based on private ownership and the use of accumulated wealth to achieve the manufacture and distribution of goods and services. Persons may do evil within this system. It may not be inherently evil, but this is disputed. State socialism is based on corporate ownership to achieve the same ends as privately owned capital. The people are the theoretical owners but the state in fact serves as the people's surrogate. Persons may do evil within this system. It is not inherently evil, but in practice it can harbor abundant evils—particularly as regards unequal distribution of private property and the violation of rights.

The moral evils attending each system, capitalist and socialist, are pointed out time and again by the other. Each tends to stress its achievements and the other's failures. The possibility of self-criticism of the system in possession is open to citizens of capitalist states. It is often not available to those in corporate or socialist states (Israel and some Scandinavian countries are exceptions).

Abuses of human rights mark many socialist and all militarily dominated states. The economies of many socialist states are such that it is easy for apostles of individualism in capitalist states to tar all of the legitimate goals of these states with the brush of communism. The one thing that comes through clearest in the current debate, as socialist states like the Soviet Union and the People's Republic of China gravitate toward more private ownership for profit, is that party drones cannot be kept from living high and allowing their inefficiencies to keep millions poor or on shopping lines. Not so easy to document is the measure in which the efficiency of a capitalist state can keep millions poor and as many millions shopping for consumer goods they do not need.

Communal Solutions Needed The fact is that the goals of any modern state for its people—such as literacy, education, nourishment, health care, employment, child care, and care for the elderly—can be accomplished only communally, that is, at the level of society. Even in cultures where the fabric of family or clan has remained strong, there is no other way in the larger society than the communal way. An important question about either system is whether human rights, including the free profession of religion, have been abridged or denied in the communal solution. This has usually been the case in states dominated by doctrinaire Marxism. The other side of this coin of repression is that among Western nations the United States ranks lowest in its support of families, particularly of women and children, and the same in the adequacy of support payments required for the children of divorce. The proportion of functional illiterates in the United States remains, at the same time, very high compared to countries it affects to look down on. The burden on all to see to the needs of all is axiomatic for Christians, not just in their church communities but in any larger society in which they have a part.

Heavy taxation of incomes, individual and corporate, is usually necessary in the modern state to achieve these communal solutions. The avoidance of taxation by legislative "loopholes" represents theft on the grand scale. Crying "Socialism!" is the first response of those who wish only to profit by societal life, not to contribute to it. The stigma of the socialist label is misdirected to any public agency (generically, the state) that knows it has an obligation to meet the needs of all.

Land Redistribution In a number of countries land redistribution has begun to be required legally after centuries of monopolistic ownership by a few. The best means to effect such redistribution and the efficacy of forcible expropriation are intensely debated, but the necessity of change in land distribution in those circumstances can hardly be debated. In the case of the three hundred leading families in a Central American republic or the somewhat greater number in the Philippines, the land needs to be taken by the state acting as the instrument of society, the people. The wealthy landowners have no clear title to their huge parcels of land, even after four hundred years. The "right of patronage" by the crown was never a license to steal. What the rich claim as "ownership" has meant the oppression and starvation of millions over many centuries. When their ill-gotten and unjustly held gains are taken from them by just political process they torch, murder, and torture. They also cry "Foul!" Sometimes their foul cry is heard, even in the highest church councils, which should heed only the cry of the poor.

The principle of enforced distribution remains viable even in a client state of the USSR like Cuba. That country's clearly documented violations of civil rights do not make immoral its thirty-year-old redistribution of the land, which was done initially in favor of the majority of the population. Its concern for universal health care, education, and the needs of the poor and its crackdown on prostitution, drugs, and gambling are moral by any standard, Christian or other.

Catholic moral teaching, at least of the last century, has enunciated in modern terms the truth that possession of the land and its resources is the right of all the people. Individuals may be made by society to forfeit the exercise of this right if there are persons deprived of their rights because of ownership in the

hands of a few. What some people call *spoliation*, Catholic morality calls *justice* if the landowners, having been told to turn large
parcels over to the landless poor, refuse. The same is true of corporations and individuals who balk at very high taxes on very
high profits or personal income. Many Catholics resist bitterly
the moral teaching of the church in this matter. They prefer to
describe this teaching on distributive justice as a capitulation to
Marxist statism, rather than calling their own practice by its
right name of nondistributive injustice.

Government's Function: To Secure Justice Ownership should
be a realistic possibility for as broad a spectrum of a population
as possible. Such is the stand taken universally by Catholic moralists. This support of private ownership, however, does not
mean that anyone has the right to unlimited accumulation of
wealth. The Catholic bishops of the United States have stated:

> Private property does not constitute for anyone an absolute
> or unconditional right. No one is justified in keeping for
> his [or her] exclusive use what he [or she] does not need,
> when others lack necessities....
>
> The...church opposes all statist and totalitarian economic
> approaches to socio-economic questions. Social life is richer
> than governmental power can encompass. All groups that
> compose society have responsibilities to respond to the de-
> mands of justice....
>
> For this reason...the teachings of the church insist that
> *government has a moral function: protecting human rights and
> securing basic justice for all members of the commonwealth.* (Ec-
> onomic Justice for All: Pastoral Letter on Catholic Social Teach-
> ing and the U.S. Economy, 1986, nos. 115, 121, 122. Emphasis
> added)

Catholic Morality as Social Catholic morality is clearly social
as much as individual. It requires of the baptized certain courses
of action that touch on the acquisition of money and possessions, but also on their distribution in society.

Governments exact moneys from their citizens that may then be allocated for public causes. They may do this in a just or an unjust manner. Surely agents of government have this option, often exercising it as a means of personal enrichment. The only way most citizens have of influencing government policies is to elect parties and politicians whose views, if put into practice, would achieve the greatest good of the greatest number. Such is the normal way for individuals to achieve the common good. More can be done, however, than exercising the voting franchise. Persons who are members of trade and professional groups, labor unions and advocacy groups, and business or financial enterprises must also act responsibly to seek the common good.

...Volunteering time, talent, and money to work for greater justice is a fundamental expression of Christian love and social solidarity. All who have more than they need must come to the aid of the poor....

Every citizen...has the responsibility to work to secure justice and human rights through an organized social response.... The guaranteeing of basic justice for all is not an optional expression of largesse but an inescapable duty for the whole of society (*ibid.*, nos. 119, 120).

Thunder from the Pulpit?

Awareness of these stern demands of morality is slow in coming because within the church, at least at local levels, they are too infrequently described as requirements of faith. Two aspects of the problem may be singled out.

The Teaching Voice The papacy has a good record as a teacher on these matters (setting aside the ambiguities of Vatican finances). So do some national bodies of bishops. The same can be said of some Catholic colleges and universities. This remains true even though the required courses in the theology and philosophy of society grow ever smaller and the compromises with wealth and the dollar search ever larger. But at least the ideal is kept alive in the few distinguished courses in social ethics that survive. In departments of economics and political science in Catholic colleges, however, the ethical demands of the Catholic faith are often disregarded. This sobering reality is often masked by a "pursuit of excellence" policy ("No values, please").

Young People: The Need for Conversion Catholic secondary schools are the setting of some remarkable efforts at consciousness-raising in morality. Often the battle is uphill for the teachers. In many cases, the parental outlook is not favorable. An adolescent who has been raised in an acquisitive household ("I never saw a consumer product I didn't like") is not a good candidate for conversion to another way of thinking except via rebellion. Peer pressures during high school years play a very strong part. The natural desire of youths to possess things of their own is an important factor. It is a part of nature but it needs education. For the young, the desire may have no outlet but dreams of possessing, and often the dreaming is constant. Many youth are earners in high school. Among these earners, many are learning the hard choices that having their own income entails. Others have a view of ownership that is in no way nuanced. They earn only to possess. The adolescents who are given much without effort are the least enviable of all. It is a terrible handicap to be raised in an environment that knows the price of everything and the value of nothing.

If these young people claim the name "Christian," they must be brought to the point of conversion—not just by adults but also through some of them helping their peers along—until it is seen that the heart of the gospel is the struggle against greed. Such conversion does not happen easily. This is a time when the young often wish to identify repression of their sexual desires as the heart of the gospel so that they can reject the gospel. They need to come face-to-face with the simple desire to acquire without regard for others' needs. This is a much more formidable adversary than the sex passion. Like faith in Christ itself, the encounter with greed entails the re-examination of all values.

A cruel paradox of the present time is that religious "conversion" is being offered to people of all ages, students especially, on an ideological basis that requires no repudiation of God's great enemy, mammon. Sometimes not too many questions are asked about sexual habits so long as one keeps mouthing Bible texts. The whole thing is a hoax and it is to be found everywhere—"conversion to Christ" without conversion to Christ.

Seeking Security in Good Conscience

The search for economic security is very much a part of today's—or any age's—life. It cannot be dismissed glibly as a lack of trust in God. Jesus taught total trust in God early and often in his ministry. His apostles and their successors did the same (see 1 Timothy 6:6–10; James 5:1–6). A teacher like Paul made clear that this trust was to be exercised through reliance on the believing community. "Always seek one another's good and, for that matter, the good of all" (1 Thessalonians 5:15b); "While we have the opportunity, let us do good to all—but especially those of the household of faith" (Galatians 6:10). Upbuild the church, Paul taught, and you will have the care of God's providence to support you. God always works through human means. Hence, the reason to rely on providence is the network of human support. This includes public welfare, that noble phrase so tragically debased.

The Church: Acting Out the Mandate The church is acting out Paul's mandate twenty centuries later by advocating the reform of structures in our society that cause or perpetuate the oppression of the poor. Through a network of diocesan organizations known generically as Catholic Charities, the church in the United States provided $535 million worth of services to more than seven million people in 1985. Separate the administration of federal funds contained in that figure, then compare it with total Catholic earning power, and the sum is painfully small. Some recent figures divulge that Lutherans, with an average congregation size of 411, give an average of $653 to their churches annually; members of the Episcopal Church, whose congregations average 476 congregants, give $599; and United Methodists give $553, the average congregation having 703 members. Catholic parishes average 3,350 members in the study cited (they count babies; not all do), and the average parishioner gives $278. The difference cannot be explained by a higher Protestant income. Catholic income is slightly higher. Direct mail appeals may be more numerous and more generously given to than the $278 figure shows. But this is an unproved hypothesis.

In 1969, the U.S. bishops with their Campaign for Human Development began to engage in a program of making Catholic people's money available for projects in antipoverty action, legal aid, voter registration, housing, and community organization. It has given grants to religious and civic causes indiscriminately on the basis of applications describing their importance. The CHD effort is one to be proud of but the ghost of $278 per person lingers.

Those who hold a particular view of government praise the spirit of volunteerism, as they call it (no tax dollars for need!), even while they consider many of the projects that are funded this way to be wrongheaded. They see government's chief task as the production of an arsenal of destructive weapons ("defense" is the euphemism) rather than the bringing about of justice. But the activists of all the churches continue their efforts to give some economic security to those who have the least, both directly and through their constant reminders of society's obligations to its members.

Intelligent Preparation Nothing can be cited from Jesus' teaching to show that preparing for security in retirement or saving for children's college fees or legislating for catastrophic illness betrays a lack of trust in God. Jesus wanted his hearers to respond to their life problems humanly, which is to say intelligently. His warnings were against living as if there were no God in the world, only human resources.

There is not an adult of any age nor a young person, paying attention to the data, who is not aware of the threat posed by economic insecurity. Life savings are often nonexistent. They can also be wiped out quickly in old age by a short but costly illness. Pension plans exist for some, certificates of deposit and mutual funds for others. Large segments of the population have heard of the first but never of the other two, and many have no realistic hope of any of these means of providing security.

How much desire and planning for security are compatible with faithful gospel living—Catholic living? It is, quite simply, incompatible with Jesus' teaching to want to ensure a greater income than is demonstrably needed. Whether the motive is to have the best of everything or to impress others or to boost a sagging confidence in oneself, such motives will not do. It has been said that old age is paranoia, and there is something to that statement. Insecurity breeds anxiety, the more so as that which once provided security dwindles. But the canker of illegitimate desire and its close relative covetousness is at work in another crowd altogether: those who want more than they need. Jesus says that the Father of all—his Father—cannot abide this in us. The reason is the same as for all human sin. Such unchecked desires will destroy us.

Saving for a rainy day, keeping an eye on life expectancy charts and the possibilities of accident, worrying about dependents unprovided for—none of these impugns a God of provident care. All are acts of reasonable forethought in a life where little is certain. The man in Jesus' parable was called a fool (Luke 12:16–21) not because he planned ahead without taking sudden death into account, but because he tore down the barns that met his needs and built new ones that did not. Being provident is a virtue. Providing for one's needs as if there were no God is a vice.

The moral dilemmas that come with trying to administer money, goods, and property are as puzzling as any in life. Jesus taught that a few basic convictions were needed in order to cope. He put it starkly: "What profit does a person show who gains the whole world and forfeits life in the process? What can anyone offer in exchange for one's life?" (Mark 8:36–37). When we go the way of acquisition unlimited it is our very selfhood that we forfeit.

There is no appreciable difference among Catholic, Protestant, and Orthodox teachings on use of possessions, despite the familiar charge that the Calvinist tradition looks on earthly prosperity as a sign of divine favor. That is a perversion of the indisputable teaching of the Reform on the virtues of industry and frugality. These are undoubtedly biblical virtues but they must be read with an eye to Jesus' openhandedness and reliance on God's providence. In Aesop's categories Jesus was neither ant nor grasshopper. He let others provide for his needs while he was engaged in an unproductive activity called preaching the gospel of salvation (see Luke 8:1–3). He had worked hard with his hands before moving on to this activity (see Mark 6:3). Like St. Paul, another hard worker (see 2 Thessalonians 3:8), Jesus would have recommended that anyone who would not work should not eat (v. 10). But his bottom line was (yes, they had ledger sheets in his day), "You have received without cost so give without charge" (Matthew 10:8b).

5

Is There More to Sex
Than the Morality
of the Body?

Newsman writes a column on the AIDS peril. Tells three stories
in rapid fire of one-night (afternoon) stands. The first features a
young naval officer in Washington who eyes a beautiful woman
hotly, exits with her to her limousine, where they promptly tear
off each other's clothes in the back seat. Afterward, introduc-
tions are exchanged. Scenario two. A woman book editor in
New York has a dinner date with a married lawyer after their
first business conference. They end up making—er—love
against the kitchen sink in her apartment. Same city, True Ro-
mances three. A teacher in his twenties picks up a redhead,
younger still, in his convertible. They repair to a quiet place but
this time the plot line is unlike the other two. Front seat. All this,
it turns out, is happening in your local three-screen movie
house, not necessarily on the same evening. The columnist is
irate. Not a peep about a condom in any of the movies because
"AIDS is a lousy love story."

"Making love" is a lousy love story much of the time it appears on our screens, whether in the local Cinema 3 or the family room during the children's hour. The journalist reporter is probably an upstanding family man, but at the moment morality is no concern of his. He may not even think it figures in the script. He just wants the dying to stop. That is not a bad thing to want.

Everyone wants the dying to stop. If we bracket the AIDS question for a bit (not to worry; it will not go away), there is time to talk about sex between a man and a woman as in the three movies above. Tumbling in the hay is as old as haystacks. "Dr. Ruth" Westheimer identifies a haystack as the scene of her first encounter as a seventeen-year-old in Israel. The Bible tells numerous such tales without featuring the awkward presence of a steering wheel or bucket seats, which make it harder.

When, much later, the early medieval moralists drew up a list of seven sins that were deadly to life in Christ they called one of them *luxuria*. Our English word—basically a German one—is "lust," meaning pleasure, delight, or desire. Without such passionate desire no baby would ever be born, not even the highest saint in heaven. In the providential design sex had to be pleasurable—or no couple, looking ahead to the pain of child-rearing, would take on the demanding obligations that followed upon an unpleasant act.

It is an animal act, that much is clear. This fact repels certain persons of both sexes who will not face their animality. It is at the same time, or can be, an act immensely attractive in prospect and satisfying in execution. Otherwise we would have an underpopulated animal kingdom—and that includes the human race.

Catholic morality on sex can be summarized briefly: wait until marriage and then let your enjoyment of sex nourish your union, for children can come of it.

This view of sex seems woefully outmoded in a culture that has separated sex from marriage almost entirely—except when a couple "decides to have a baby." In this century more than in any other, sex has become an independent pleasure totally distinct from childbearing and even marriage. The contraception industry, with the pill in the lead, is a heavy contributor to this view. But, it may be questioned, did the protective devices bring about the rush to pleasure, or was it the other way around? All of these devices were developed with a view primarily to the married consumer, but the larger market cannot have escaped the notice of the manufacturers. In recent times it has provided the bulk of their trade.

The Separation of Sex and Marriage

The whole issue of the separation of sex from marriage is so complex that one would be foolhardy to isolate a single factor in its development. If any factors have to be identified as the leading ones, they would probably be the loosened bonds of the tightly knit kinship family and the fact that in our culture children are no longer economic assets but liabilities.

Passion will rage in the human frame (that is passion's business, after all), and reason and religious conviction will try to get the upper hand until the last day. But once unlimited opportunity for sex is available, the contest becomes unequal. The last barrier to fall is social sanction. The moment society stops saying that sex outside of marriage (one's own marriage) is sin, injustice, or reprehensible conduct, but says instead that sex is available to everyone in the normal course of things regardless of state, then sex outside marriage begins to "happen" more and more. The abnormal becomes the normal, the unusual the usual.

But the laws of human biology continue to operate. So do the laws of the human heart. People are hurt terribly by recreational sex, starting with the people who are aborted as a result of it or are born of it. Some are led to think that love is behind these illicit sexual acts and learn to their regret that such is never the case. Some, too, become deadened to the possibility of love or marriage by their endless search for "perfect sex."

Religious people whose traditions include a sexual ethos— that is to say, most religious people—are carried along in this global tide like the rest. Their leaders and teachers wonder whether the commitment to chastity within and outside marriage is so fragile that it may not be able to be passed on to coming generations. Is anyone listening when the sexual morality of Catholics and Christians generally, which derives from that of the Jews of the Bible, is described as God's way for humanity?

The Biblical Perspective

Ancient Israel What is God's way for humanity and how does anyone know it? The Bible deals with sex very matter-of-factly. For the biblical authors, it is a human "given." The Jewish Scriptures convey no fear of it, no fulminating against it. The assumption is that most humans will marry and that most couples will bear children. Preventing births was not a biblical problem, although every sort of abortifacient and contraceptive method was known to the ancient world. The Israelites (later the "Jews") looked on offspring as a sign of God's favor. Despite wars and famines, this people did not abort fetuses, approve of interfering with the sex act once it had been begun, or destroy unwanted infants by exposure. They were like many other of the world's peoples in that respect.

The Israelites' covenanted status with their God, the LORD, gave them an added incentive to keep their population strong. Ancient Israel saw much death in childbirth. It was likewise familiar with adultery and sex between the unmarried. It kept affirming the goodness of sex between the married for the sake of offspring and its unacceptability in any other circumstances.

Jesus: A Sexual Morality of Personalism Jesus' only recorded words on adultery were to declare that the lustful male gaze is the equivalent of the deed. He meant by this the intent to "have" a woman if circumstances would allow it. He also forbade the repudiation of women by their husbands for any cause.

Notice that in both cases, the root cause of the evil deed is injustice. The sin consists in stealing the wife or the daughter of another, even with a leer. It is thought morally evil to set a woman adrift so that her life as "damaged goods" becomes hard or impossible. Jesus' sexual morality is identical with that of the Bible. This biblical code does not speculate on the nature of the sexual act, although it is convinced it knows what is natural. The code has no theories about what should go where and when. It is not a morality of *physicalism*. Jesus and the biblical tradition have a sexual morality of *personalism*. No person is to be used as an object, mere chattel, not even in a time when slavery was a social institution. Sexual sin is such for one reason only—namely, that some person or persons are being violated in their human rights. Not only is their full personhood not being respected but the peoplehood of all is being damaged. Sexual sin is always social, never merely individual. In the case of Christians in the early communities, the spreading abroad of the Spirit in their hearts made the offense far more heinous one for them.

Saint Paul: Mutual Conjugal Rights The concern for justice was the framework that Saint Paul used when he dealt with issues of human sexuality. He described conjugal rights as mutual. Neither husband nor wife has a greater claim on the body-person of the spouse than the other (see 1 Corinthians 7:2–5). The special problem that he addressed in that letter was an ascetical abstention from sex which one of the partners was finding beyond his or her strength. The only sexual abstinence Paul actively counseled, unlike his confused Corinthians, was from immorality (see also 1 Thessalonians 4:3). What he called permissible abstention was that agreed upon for a time so that both could "devote themselves to prayer." Both persons, in seeking the salvation that is God's will, should gain mastery over their bodies (or, in the case of 1 Thessalonians 4:4, "live with his spouse"—the words in the original can have both meanings) and not give in to passion like the heathen. Fidelity to one's partner is the chief guarantee against passion's leading a person into other paths. The reason Paul gave for the sinfulness of adultery was that it is a disregard of God and the gift of the Holy Spirit. Both the self and fellow believers are the ones directly involved. The more immediate reason that a man's adulterous act is immoral is that it does wrong to the cheated spouse by invading that other's rights. The rights of the woman with whom the man commits adultery are trampled on too, but the theft is from the offended husband.

Paul had no corresponding discussion of sexual sin by the unmarried. The ancient Jewish world was almost universally acquainted with early and arranged marriages and with protected females. This meant that much premarital sex, not all, had the character of rape.

St. Paul cannot readily be accused of thinking of the wife as a possession. He knew well the ways of men in the double-standard pagan culture of Corinth, where relapse into the extramarital satisfaction of former ways beckoned strongly. He spoke against the men's sins of passion in which their wives were the victims. Paul even framed an argument against their patronizing the prostitutes of their pre-Christian days that hinged on the prostitutes' human dignity. Disregarding the male tendency to hold prostitutes cheap—mere pawns of pleasure for pay. Paul identified such sexual unions as a matter of becoming "one body with her" on a par with marriage (1 Corinthians 6:16). The offending males were guilty of a sin against the Spirit because they sinned against persons in whom the Spirit can dwell.

Through the Centuries

Has the church as church never been confused in its teaching on sexuality? The observations above sound as if the writer thinks not. The case is otherwise. Saint Paul seems to have been an incurable widower or bachelor who freely shared his prejudices in favor of the single life—making clear, however, that his state was not suited to many (1 Corinthians 7:25–35). His views, it seems, did little in his day to multiply the number of the celibate. That came later. Remarrying after widowhood was frowned on in the early centuries of the church, but that perspective had other roots than the New Testament. The Judaism of the period similarly disfavored it, possibly under Platonic-Stoic influence. The church absorbed from pagan philosophies the idea that any exercise of passion was somehow ignoble. This meant that abstention from sex and the other passions was superior to yielding to them. Such unbiblical teaching made early inroads because of the attractiveness Stoic self-control had for Christians.

As early as the turn of the second century, sharp warnings began to appear against the boastfulness of sexually continent church leaders who compared themselves favorably to the married (1 Clement 38:2; Ignatius to Polycarp 5:2). A century later people were found to be preferring the ministrations of monks and celibate clergy over married clergy. This forced bishops to demand that their people accept the spiritual services of their married clergy, themselves among them. The same philosophical shrinking from the "carnal" as described above was at work here. Its positive side was a gravitation toward ascetics who could control themselves, as ordinary people found they could not. Control of passion had become the great virtue, yielding to it even in marriage a sign of weakness. Only much later was a positive asceticism of sexual abstention for the sake of the service of the gospel or greater freedom for prayer developed.

At the same time, the church inherited from postbiblical Judaism the mentality that engaging in sex to beget children was the good that justified the act. (The pagans were thought to avail themselves of sex because they wallowed in lust—see an expression of this perspective in Tobit 8:7.) This view of the place of sex in marriage took hold early in the church and died hard. The youthful Manichaean Augustine (354–430 C.E.) never entirely put behind him his contempt for sex in principle and his shame over yielding to it with a mistress for over fifteen years. Throughout his Confessions, in full maturity as a bishop, he never expresses regret at his grave injustice in not asking this woman to be his wife. In total male narcissism he deplores only his yielding to passion. Augustine's personal "weakness" seems to have led him to the rationale that sex of its nature has the character of sin. The excess of passion over reason, he taught, is justified only by the intention to have a child. Since the force of passion in intercourse in some measure always escapes the control of grace-filled reason (he went on), sinful concupiscence accompanies every sexual act. This was his explanation of the way "original sin"—to which he gave its name—was transmitted: physically. This particular perspective of Augustine did not become the official teaching of the church, neither the sinfulness of concupiscence nor the mode of transmission of hereditary sin. Most seminary courses have not featured this chapter of patristic teaching for a long time. It comes as a surprise to many priests to learn it. Feminist researchers often bring it to the attention of priests for the first time. But even though these views did not become official church teaching, Augustine cast a long shadow in the West. Clergy and laity alike are unconsciously tainted by his Manichaean views. You may say that he lost the battle but won the war, if "won" is a correct description for such widespread human loss. We are talking about a suspicion of sex as shameful in even the holiest of conjugal circumstances.

Vatican Council II: An Affirmation of Sexuality

Only at Vatican Council II was it finally stated unequivocally in a church document—after fifteen centuries of Augustinian domination in the West—that

married love is uniquely expressed and perfected by the exercise of the acts proper to marriage. Hence the acts in marriage by which the intimate and chaste union of the spouses takes place are noble and honorable; the truly human performance of these acts fosters the self-giving they signify and enriches the spouses in joy and gratitude. (*Gaudium et Spes* [The Church in the Modern World], No. 49)

Later in the document, the council stated:

But marriage is not merely for the procreation of children: its nature as an indissoluble contract between two people and the good of the children demand that the mutual love of the partners be properly shown, that it should grow and mature. Even in cases where, despite the intense desire of the spouses there are no children, marriage still retains its character of being a whole manner and communion of life and preserves its value and indissolubility (No. 50).

Despite their veiled language, those statements are affirmations of the importance, and joy, of sex in both fruitful and childless marriages. Sex is of the essence of the married state.

Brutal sex, however, is not of the essence of marriage. When, some years ago, the present pope—in one of a long series of midday talks on family life—spoke of the possibility of rape in marriage, there was a surprising outcry against his utterance. Perhaps it was thought that, as the first bishop of the Catholic communion, he was traditionally ill at ease with sex in marriage as a couple's unqualified right. What the pope was doing, of course, was qualifying the right importantly, saying that women have a right not to be violated forcibly even within marriage. Everyone knows that sexual activity is a perfectly legitimate human activity, the protest seemed to say. Let no celibate pope express his squeamishness about an activity he probably disapproves of anyway!

Sex and Parenthood

The sections from the council document quoted above and the section following them are about the relationship of sex to parenthood. They underscore the unbroken Catholic tradition that abortion and infanticide are "abominable crimes." At the same time the bishops in council teach that parenthood should be embarked on "with a sense of human and Christian responsibility and the formation of correct judgments—through docile respect for God, and common reflection and effort" (No. 50). The teaching of *Gaudium et Spes* continues:

"[Parenthood] also involves a consideration of their own

good and the good of their children already born or yet to come, an ability to read the signs of the times and of their own situation on the material and spiritual level, and, finally, an estimation of the good of the family, of society, and of the church" (No. 50).

It is clear from this that the conception of children in marriage is placed solidly on a social basis. The failure of a couple to act responsibly about the children they do and do not bring into the world offends against their own humanity, against the whole race, and against the body of Christ.

As part of this social burden, the document says, not only must good intention and the evaluation of motives be taken into account but also "objective criteria." These criteria are to be drawn from "the nature of the human person and human action." They are described as criteria that "respect the total meaning of mutual self-giving and human procreation in the context of true love" (No. 5l). With a conscientious view to these norms of gospel-oriented and human behavior, "it is the married couple themselves who must in the last analysis arrive at these judgments before God" (No. 50).

This teaching of the world's Catholic bishops in council is the traditional teaching. Popes and bishops and couples before and after it simply reflect it. Since Pius XI's 1930 encyclical letter *On Chaste Marriage*, the papal interpretation of that conciliar teaching on this matter has concentrated on one objective criterion, namely the way the sex act is performed. Performance is given precedence over the other considerations in the total nature of marriage. Catholic couples with increasing frequency have seen that the delicate relationship and the economics of the married state place heavy burdens on them. Sustained or periodic abstention from sex has proved to be an additional burden. Papal teaching of the last sixty years is beyond doubt the official teaching of the church. It describes not only contraception in marriage but each individual contraceptive act as objectively sinful. The offense is situated not in society or in the family but in the act itself, with the teaching that nature demands that the act once begun must be completed.

The resistance to this one aspect of the papal teaching by married Catholics, who by their continued childbearing prove they are against contraception as a general program for marriage, is called in theological language its "nonreception." This widespread reality has so pre-empted discussion of the question that the basic agreement on it between the two parties trying to say something to each other has been obscured. Married Catholics have largely received the church's tradition against contraception. They have not received a specification of it which calls the unhindered completion of all sex acts preferable to every other good of marriage.

The agreement between pope and people is that the begetting of children must be responsibly planned with a view to available economic and emotional resources. The disagreement is over the availability of those resources and what to do in the conduct of marriage given their unavailability. Both women and men in marriage know they have human responsibilities and callings besides that of being child-begetters. The latter responsibility is grave but it is not the only one. Selfish avoidance of it, whether by natural or artificial means, can be a sin against both the marriage and society. On that you find general agreement, although those who avoid conception by natural means other than abstention ("rhythm," "natural family planning") tend not to stress the question of motive. The physical approach to the problem understandably finds a physical answer satisfactory.

In the church's teaching, sex is a good of marriage and marriage is the proper place for sex. It is not morally good in any other setting. Child-rearing is a long and demanding process. The risk of conception and childbearing should not be embarked on by any couple not prepared to accept the responsibilities of child-rearing. This is true whether the couple is unmarried or the parents of many. The technology of birth regulation by natural and artificial means alike is relatively so advanced—however widely it is disregarded—that the culture we inhabit is prone to say that sex and parenthood are totally separate human activities, because they can in fact be separated. But although the separation is a technical reality and brings with it less physiological risk all the time, it is rendered humanly impossible by the laws of the human heart. Sex and conception may be separable by technical means, but the psychic harm that sex partners who use such techniques can visit on each other proves that this is not a damage-free situation. The medical evidence on whether contraception consistently engaged in causes permanent physiological harm to the woman still has some inconclusive features. There remains the question of the harm done to the human relationship, and the fact that abortion may be resorted to when the contraceptive measures that were so confidently relied on fail.

The Cultural Context
The teachings of the Catholic tradition on sexuality—not too long ago those of the entire Christian tradition—are thought by the surrounding culture to be fraught with absurdity. A number of pragmatic axioms are proposed to put to rout this "unrealistic" idealism of the Catholic teaching. They include the following: "Teenagers are going to be sexually active no matter what. Somehow you have to stop babies having babies." "Economically and in terms of maturity, early marriage makes less and less sense. But the sexual urge in the young is totally unaffected by these considerations." "There is a mystique of 'true love' abroad that will be used to justify extramarital sex no matter what anybody says." "The emotional and financial strain on parents is so great nowadays that large families are the burden of the poor and the luxury of the comfortable." "The AIDS threat is so massive that condoms all around is the only truly moral response."

A Corporate Answer Needed
To try to respond to any of this popular wisdom in a short space, not to say all of it, would be folly. The one word of Christian wisdom that can be spoken is this: Without corporate

action by the whole church in the midst of a culture operating on other principles, people of any age, married or single, cannot fulfill the demands of the gospel. Young people left on their own in a sea of parental silence-with-censure cannot swim against a powerful tide. The parents of families of any size, left as isolated units to work out their parental and sexual salvation, will go under almost as quickly as the young. They already doubt the wisdom of certain church teachings about sexuality in their own regard. They may be permitted to wonder about the teaching proposed regarding their children. Worst of all, the blanket of silence in the church following *Humanae Vitae*, except for papal reiteration of its distinguishing characteristic at full strength, is all-pervasive. Except for the papal censure of abortion and of contraception in all conjugal sex acts without distinction or qualification, there is sadly little moral discourse on contraceptive practice by Catholics. This has led to the omission of discussion of a wide range of moral matters and is highly injurious to the life of the whole church.

The acquiescence of Christians in the juridical doctrine of the "right to privacy," which is a commonplace, needs to be resisted corporately. This doctrine suggests without saying it that no sexual behavior has any consequences that society needs to attend to publicly. But this is quite wrong as public policy because it is wrong as public morality. There cannot be a more central issue for the public good than population, both as to quantity and quality. The existence of families, however constituted, means that the general populace has a very large stake in families, how they come to be and continue in existence.

Is it possible to exist as a family without enforced fragmentation by economic forces? How much of a threat is posed to stable families by the birth of unwanted children, in or out of wedlock? What type of ideal about sexuality can be passed along by parents who, in childhood, were given a thoroughly bad ideal or none at all? Anywhere you apply pressure to the question of human sexuality, you touch a social, not an individual, nerve. Yet the conventional wisdom—that sex is a

private affair—grows stronger, not weaker. The cost of this conviction in dollars alone is staggering.

The whole church, not just its teachers, knows that an individualist approach to sex is unreal. Yet people of all ages and
both sexes, in and out of family situations, are taught about sex
and family life as if they could cope with massive social forces
singly or as isolated families. The sex education that has a
chance to be listened to and to have an impact is not one of official church pronouncements heard on news media, or of public
education that informs "how to do it without getting caught" by
pregnancy or infection. Rather, the sex education that will make
a difference in one large segment of the population is one of total, grace-enlivened frankness in the Catholic family, parish, and
church school. It is an approach that speaks early and often of
the treasure of sex and the lifelong and life-threatening consequences that can result when it is used in wrong circumstances.
The discussion must be very open, very specific, and constant.
Young Catholics need to hear early and often why their present
happiness depends on total abstinence from sex before they
marry. The married must become convinced that contraception
as a consistent practice is inimical to their married happiness. At
the moment no such widespread discussion is taking place, only
prohibitions without adequate reasons. The use of the gift of sex
needs to be widely perceived as healthy and good by a gospel
standard. At the moment, nothing like the above is happening.

Silence as the Enemy

Our society witnesses much early resort to sex—not because it is
spoken against but because it is not spoken of seriously at all
and because, visually and by spoken innuendo, it is represented
as immensely pleasurable. The gales of laughter by studio audiences at the most casual whimsy regarding sex betray our ongoing incapacity to deal with it maturely. In and out of Catholic
life, the adult conspiracy of silence is the great enemy of people
of all ages. The silence has been shattered lately by the death

threat posed by AIDS. Up until five years ago viral diseases transmissible by sexual contact like gonorrhea, syphilis, and herpes were coped with clinically and referred to in public as diseases other people had. AIDS has changed all that. Total abstention from casual sex and needle-injected drugs is the surest preventitive. It is interesting to see how the second is being dealt with as a grave social hazard and the first as a private right. The latter being the case, condom use becomes a private obligation. There is a kind of shrinking in horror from acknowledging that any sexual behavior might have such serious public consequences that it might have to be met publicly. But it is not enough for religious believers committed to chastity in sex and abstention from drugs to deplore public policy. They need to show by their conduct that they respect life by doing nothing to threaten it.

The compassionate care of sufferers from AIDS without censure is surely a major challenge in our day, putting before us the age-old gospel question: "Who, then, is my neighbor?"

Because the pope and the bishops speak of sex publicly and always in a certain vein, they are thought to be censorious meddlers. "These are highly private matters," some sex educators say. "Only those pruriently absorbed in what is not their personal concern could address them so forcefully and repressively." Although the teachers in the church may not always express themselves in the most felicitous way, they speak for a long tradition that has the public good to the fore. If they are making applications of the gospel tradition to specific situations that the tradition does not seem to demand, they need to learn that from the people. Until such representations by the people are made clearly and with good theological and social arguments, the tradition that was valid in an age of high infant mortality will continue in possession.

The "Love That Justifies All"

When faithful Catholic married people resist the tradition of their church on sexual practice, the most usual reason they give is that love, both conjugal and parental, impels them to do so. Because love is the highest value in Christian life, this objection must be taken seriously. The mutual love of spouses brings children into existence and sustains them until they are young adults on their own. Love is a costly affair. It requires great sacrifices, hard choices both against the self and in favor of the other and all in the family.

When individuals or a couple, whether of different sexes or the same, claim love as the justification for their action within or outside marriage, they must be taken seriously. Is love the primary motivation: self-giving, other-regarding love which is the love the gospel speaks of? If it is not, what is? For the couple could it be two self-loves, two cases of selfishness? Since few motives exist in isolation, they need to be sorted out.

When an unmarried man and woman or a boy and a girl have sex, typically they say that their love requires this expression. Most often, however, if the mutual love were true it would demand restraint. Lapses of passion are understandable but they are not the same as sustained claims to a right. Sexual union in an unmarried condition causes human damage in all directions. The only case thinkable where love justifies intercourse between unmarried persons is when such intercourse occurs at an early stage in a lifetime love. In such case this consummation itself constitutes marriage.

By no means is the recognition of such a reality a counsel to disregard church law. Neither does it encourage the folly of an earlier day, when two who had brought about conception were joined forcibly in marriage. It is an acknowledgment that the sexual union of two individuals is so profound a mutual commitment of their whole persons that they are ready to be a family by this act. Indeed, most peoples on earth view this first solemn consummation as marriage, as did the church in its early centuries. Publicly given consent was simply the preliminary to consummation.

When young people are pressed as to whether this is what they intended by the sexual expression of their love, they are often puzzled by the question. What they meant to do by having sex was to discover whether the affection the one felt for the other was mutual—nothing more. Putting their action in such a serious and long-term context fills them with dismay. The term "making out" describes accurately what they had in mind—trying to make something out about themselves. But not very much. Does one esteem the other well enough, they wonder, to sustain the other's ego (and one's own) by this act? Could the other be induced—the uglier word is seduced—to capitulate to charm, blandishments, or pressure? That is all that was intended. Nothing more.

When two persons of the same sex say they are "lovers," they may be employing the word in the same cheapened sense in which it is used for heterosexual sex. And because sex apart from marriage is generally thought to be everyone's right, gays and lesbians argue that they are discriminated against by not being free to do what heterosexuals do freely. "He/she is my lover" means my current sex partner (although it may mean more). The heterosexual language is taken over.

The much more serious question is that of two persons of the same sex who love each other in a fully personal and complete way. So much is this the case that they wish to share a life together until one dies. This love may be questioned, like any love, but the proof of it is the sacrifice and mutual caring that marks it—like any love. The church has known many such friendships over its long life and has never censured them. The church has often been called "homophobic" in recent times for saying what it has always said—that genital excitement or intercourse apart from marriage is not morally available to any couple, regardless of sex. This is a hard saying for people who are unattracted by the married state. It is the same for the married who do not love their spouses or are not loved by them. It is just as hard for those who have freely committed themselves to one another but whose state is incompatible with marriage.

Intense pain is experienced everywhere as a result of the confinement of sexual expressions of love to the state of marriage.

Gay- and lesbian-oriented persons are often reminded in thoughtless or cruel ways of the restraints governing all baptized persons. They demand to have what they see all others free to have, or so it appears—an active sex life with another person. With one other? For life? With a person for whom parenthood is a desire and a possibility? The widespread disregard by heterosexual Christians of the demands of the gospel on their lives as sexual beings has made the hard life of the homosexually oriented even more difficult.

The conditions of active sex for a Catholic (or a Muslim, a Jew, a Hindu, or a Buddhist) are extremely circumscribed. They are nothing short of a heroic demand. How people fulfill this demand is God's business and theirs *and the community's*. Catholics (among others) are aided in their sex lives by the grace of Christ. But unless this grace is expressed through the support of a network of believers and available over a long and hard lifetime, it simply will not be available. God works through human beings.

When Venus and Caritas Christi Meet

There are so many cases and so few easy answers. A man and a woman are widowed. Federal tax legislation makes marriage a penalty situation. So they live together without getting married. A couple is married at law but one of them is not canonically free to be married sacramentally. Both have long regretted their non-eucharistic Catholic lives, reckoning the loss almost greater than the benefit of their life together. But it seems unjust to the other to terminate the marriage, even morally wrong; so they do not. And they wait.

Two young persons come to love each other dearly. They are free to enter into a sacramental marriage, and they may even wish to, hope to. But one or the other—sometimes both—are unsure. So they move in with each other to find out. Is a lifetime commitment as terrifying as it seems? Is the other person as satisfying to be with in every mood and tense as it seemed would be the case in their happiest times together? Is there enough money between them to make marriage possible? These are serious questions in the mind of one or both.

Perhaps, however, one or the other is not fully serious, thinking: "There is the door. I can always get out of this." That dark shadow hangs over an otherwise happy union. It is often built not on an active lack of trust so much as on an inability to trust. Everything in life up to this point has made one or the other psychologically unfit for a lifetime commitment. Do they sin while they live together and stop sinning the day of their Catholic marriage four years later? There has to be another vocabulary to describe this confused psychological state.

The whole believing community tends to leave answers to those questions to the pair of any age and to God. It may speak of objective right and wrong in the case, but passing judgments on confused minds and turbulent hearts is something that usually is not done. Too often the believing community leaves couples like these adrift: "They know what they're doing." "I tried to talk to them once but it was useless." Often those who most love such persons find themselves unable to assist. Or they step in to help in the most unhelpful way imaginable. But the church as a community of people usually does not try. Individual choice is allowed to prevail yet another time. The couple in question is in need of basic church support and they do not receive it.

We end as we began. There seems to be such a thing as sex, defined as a union of bodies. Foreplay. Coitus—intercourse. In reality, there is no such thing. There is only a union of persons. These are persons with an eternal destiny—but just as importantly, a temporal one. In most cases they are capable of transmitting life to other persons by this deed, this act. The union has consequences that can last for generations; alternatively, the consequences can be thought of as confined to one more scar on the psyche. Which will it be? How will the whole church act toward its members who are faced with questions of sex and marriage that their forebears never faced? A good start is to understand something of this mysterious gift and then to tell anyone who will listen—yes, from the housetops. The reason is that ignorance of gospel values, the prime enemy of human happiness in the mystery of sexuality, is everywhere.

6

Is There More to the Morality of the Body Than Sex?

St. Francis of Assisi referred to his body as "Brother Ass." The designation was not as uncomplimentary as it sounds. It had nothing to do with stupidity or stubbornness but with bearing life's burdens—a generally kind service rendered by the body. We still have the term "workhorse," even though the people who have ever seen one grow fewer every day. Life in medieval Italy would have been unthinkable without the ass, that uncomplaining "jack-of-haul-trades." To suppose that Francis was scorning the body by referring to it in this way is to miss the point entirely. He was praising that marvelous instrument of spirit without which there is no human life on earth.

Care for Our Bodies
The author of the Letter to the Ephesians said that "husbands should love their wives as they do their own bodies. He who

loves his wife loves himself. Observe that no one ever hates his own flesh; no, he nourishes it and takes care of it..." (Ephesians 5:28–29). The author went on to make his main point—that Christ cherishes the church in just the same way. One could say cynically that the sentiment expressed is male vanity at work, nothing more—the writer is tossing off the ignoble axiom that men think of their wives as extensions of themselves. That interpretation would seem to miss the force of his illustrative figure completely. The sacred writer was talking about the natural instinct of self-preservation, whether in a man or a woman. He could count on the unarguable proposition that people do not normally set out to destroy themselves. No one should say that the ancient world did not experience any self-destructive behavior or despair. It was there, in plenty. But in the Jewish world and the pagan circles influenced by it (like those for whom the expositor of Saint Paul's thought wrote Ephesians), life and health were great goods. This was the axiom that the writer could count on as having wide acceptance. Because all of us have an interest in our well-being, he wrote, our spouses should be cherished as dearly as we take care of our own bodies. You can scarcely call this a revealed truth. It is a truism that people live by.

In another sense, though, it is a truism that people do not live by, however well they know its truth. People eat too much (the people who have the luxury of enough to eat). They drink too much. They do not eat healthfully. They do not sleep enough—at least some do not, during certain times in their lives. Others sleep too much. People flog and maltreat Brother Ass as no poor farmer or tradesman would do to a beast that was his livelihood. The difference is that people—we—often do it to the body, which is our life.

You will not find treatises on health and safety or tips on achieving longevity in the Bible. There is no counsel on good diet and regular exercise. But warnings against the evils of taking a human life are there, as are heavy penalties for the results of carelessness or contrived damage done to others.

For instance, kidnapers were liable to the death penalty in ancient Israel (Exodus 21:16). Compensation had to be made for the enforced idleness that followed a blow that put someone out of commission. The injured one's complete recovery likewise had to be paid for (21:18–19). If a pregnant woman was injured in a male brawl and miscarried the guilty one had to be fined, the woman's husband setting the price (21:22). For the injuries she sustained, compensation in kind was required, "'eye for eye, tooth for tooth, hand for hand, foot for foot...'" (21:24). Injury to a slave that resulted in the loss of an eye or a tooth led to the slave's being freed (21:26–27). The owner of a mean or destructive ox had to pay, as did the careless landowner into whose uncovered cistern an animal wandered; so did the thief of another's sheep or ox (21:28–37).

This all sounds rather primitive, but modern claims of indemnity at law read much the same. In ancient times as now human life destroyed was irrecoverable and maiming was irreversible. But a lifetime of economic loss could often be repaid. If it could not, the damage could be testified to by a maiming that did not exceed the original injury. Call it cruel if you will, but it was a controlled cruelty, not a wanton one. The importance of the body and its members was acknowledged daily in this scheme of damages. The life of persons was their livelihood. Everyone believed that to be fully effective you had to be whole. There was not much concern for the handicapped in the ancient world, aside from the care shown for them by family and friends.

In our own time we have not progressed much beyond or even as far as these realizations. Consider, for example, our public outcries for the return of capital punishment. We want the guilty to suffer by paying the "supreme penalty" but we do not have a matching concern for the innocent—not the victims of their crimes but innocent people generally. Consider our tolerance of officeholders and lawyers who make a mockery of the OSHA (Occupational Safety and Health Administration) requirements that are built into law. We see among us much callous disregard by plant owners for the health and safety of workers. We condemn some people regularly to black lung disease, cancer from radiation and emphysema from asbestos, because the cleanup of air and other types of pollution would cost too much. A group of Catholic businesspersons, headquartered in the midwest, complain to the Secretary of the Environmental Protection Agency that stiff federal regulations regarding asbestos removal from public buildings, including Catholic schools, are too burdensome. Profits are put before lives.

On another front, the destruction of the body by alcohol, biblical morality is firmly opposed to drunkenness. It takes no stand against wine (in that predistillation age). A variety of cruelties perpetrated by men in drunken states is spelled out in the Jewish Scriptures. Biblically we begin to hear of chronic alcoholism only with the Christian writings. Neither a bishop nor a deacon may be addicted to drink, says 1 Timothy 3:3, 8. On the widespread vice of drunkenness, see Titus 1:7, Ephesians 5:18, and 1 Thessalonians 5:7.

Orgies are ruled out in the Christian writings (see Galatians 5:21 and 1 Peter 4:3). The Second Letter of Peter gets very specific about animal-like human behavior (2:12) and "afternoon delight," first-century style (2:13). Twentieth-century Christians engage in no disgusting behavior that these early writings have not already described and condemned. The swilling of beer that ends in seduction and highway death had not yet been developed as an art form in ancient times. But the early Christians seem to have been no less adept at self-destruction than we are, given the descriptions of their behavior in various New Testament strictures.

Keeping the Sanctuary Fit for Its Guest

The main deterrent to abuse of the body proposed by Saint Paul is an instructive one: "You must know that your body is a temple of the Holy Spirit, who is within—the Spirit you have received from God. You are not your own. You have been purchased, and at a price! So glorify God in your body" (1 Corinthians 6:19–20).

The context of Paul's remarks was illicit sex, but the church has never confined the interpretation of this passage to unchaste conduct. The body is a temple of the Holy Spirit at all times, not only when it is involved in the reproductive act. The times of eating and drinking, sleeping and waking are not nearly so intermittent, and they are much more insistent. A temple is a holy place because of what goes on there. The Spirit of God, in Paul's figure, is a sanctifying presence that goes down into the joints and the marrow of the body-self. There is no tiny fissure of the cortex, no follicle of hair on skin or scalp that this Spirit does not penetrate.

Most people have heard of the marvelous recuperative powers of the human organism. Ask any physiologist or neighborhood doctor what the body does to renew and repair itself once the germs inimical to it or the cells gone wild within it have been killed or excised. "I don't heal anybody," an honest physician will say. "I try to discover what is wrong, eliminate the adverse conditions, and let the body heal itself."

Generally speaking, most persons are not nearly so respectful of the body as are practitioners of the healer's art. We neglect proper bodily care, disregard the signs of the body's disintegration, and then call on a wise doctor to reverse the results of our folly. The advertising game, which has developed our national self-deceit to a high art, puts things delicately so that we will not be insulted and fail to buy the product: "For those times when you may have overindulged...." Overindulged! Not, "For those times when you were staggering drunk at a fraternity party...,"or "For those times at a Sunday brunch when you took the sign 'All you can eat' as a personal challenge." The phrase "when you may have overindulged" suits much better our tendency to rationalize.

Catholic morality has always called gluttony and drunkenness serious sins. Catholics are not noted as a class for their avoidance of either or both. Such sins are an offense against the body in whom the Spirit dwells, the profaning of a holy place.

As in all such cases, only God and the individual know when sin has been committed. Chronic conditions connected with such choices may not themselves be sinful. The anorexic adolescent or adult, for example, is striving desperately for a "good figure" but something psychologically much deeper is going on here. The same is true of a bulimic youth who takes to "pigging out" and immediately inducing vomiting as a means of coping with some intolerable life situation. People in these two conditions do not set out to profane the body. The profaning can be the unintended result of a series of unwise decisions made with wholly different goals or pressures in mind. The same is true of alcoholism and addiction to licit or illicit drugs. Few people begin an addiction by intending to destroy themselves. Destruction overtakes them. A physical predisposition to alcoholism may be in the genes (this has largely been established as a fact), or there may be a predisposition deriving from the pattern of family life. No one warns the victim-to-be. Often the persons most in a position to give a warning are least capable of doing so.

Warnings go unheeded: "What, me an alcoholic? I'm only nineteen. Besides, I'm just having fun with the guys." Early warning signals are present. The person often feels silly or lightheaded when drinking and knows that he or she is talking too much or too loudly. The individual wants to be where alcohol is served, is the first one to suggest getting a six-pack or a keg. The drinker might not be sure what someone said to him or her the night before. Or the person may have a foggy remembrance of sexual familiarity the previous evening even if she or he thinks it did not "go all the way."

Today in this country we have reached the point where highway billboards and bumper stickers say, "Don't drink and drive." The vigilance of MADD (Mothers Against Drunk Driving) members has a lot to do with this and SADD (Students) is the follow-up. Often these mothers are Rachels weeping for their children, "for they are not."

We have not progressed, however, as far as erecting billboards that say, "Don't drink too much. It could kill you." Or, "Don't drink and have sex." Those are still thought to be matters of privacy. The tragedy of eight teenagers wiped out in a head-on crash is considered a public question, but the phenomenon of conceiving new life in an alcoholic haze has not yet become a public concern. Many think that the Supreme Court decision allowing abortion needs to stand, among other reasons, precisely so that we can have it handy to correct our "private" follies.

Catholic morality knows no such distinction: "Shun lewd conduct. Every other sin a person commits is outside his body, but the fornicator [read: gormandizer, drunk] sins against his own body" (1 Corinthians 6:18), a body in which the Holy Spirit dwells.

Any Exculpation for the Toxic?

When we consider the issue of drinking and responsibility we are in deep waters. What is the morality of an action in which great harm is done—like killing others in a car crash or begetting new life while semiconscious—when freedom of choice is so diminished that people can say, "I was so far gone I didn't know what I was doing"? The claim is constantly being made in the courts. Presidential counselor Michael Deaver's claim in his perjury trial of 1987 was that his alcoholism should have exculpated him. Juries are asked to pass judgment regularly on this claim. Unscrupulous lawyers—always the minority—coach their clients to claim a blackout when in fact they remember that they insisted on driving or that they reached for the kitchen knife. "We were having a few beers [fourteen!]. After that, I don't remember much of anything."

The Catholic moral tradition does not say who is or is not guilty before God. But the tradition maintains that to choose freely the diminishment of the powers of mind or memory is to be responsible for what follows. Quite clearly, many criminal or morally reprehensible acts occur of which the performer has no memory. Persons are morally obliged to think ahead of the consequences of freely choosing to lessen their acumen of sense or judgment, the tradition says. They *have to* look down the road.

Befuddled persons are the worst monitors in the world of their own actions. Their whole previous history, mental and emotional, goes into the choice of getting into this state. That history may have been chaotic. At a certain point of intake they are out of control. Rage, jealousy, and drink rob them of their freedom.

Take a man who has had too much to drink at a party. His friends know it. The signs are familiar. At that point friendship—perhaps family membership as well—imposes heavy burdens. Someone has to take the car keys away from Mr. Macho, forcibly if necessary. The bartender is under a moral obligation not to serve him another drink. The gang may have to take him home and deposit him on his doorstep. None of us finds anything charming about seeing a drunk safely home. But we are talking of human lives here, that of the drunk and of the people he might kill or injure before the night is over.

Alcohol as the drug of choice is on the increase in colleges and among youth of high school age. Drugs, even soft drugs, are decreasing in those populations, but crack is soaring in the ghetto and cocaine-snorting is holding its own among the affluent, depending on the stability of "the Market." The basic fact here is that experimentation, even with pot, can be deadly. This is not a question of whether soft drugs lead to hard by a law of physiology. It is a matter of wanting to see what a greater high might be like and already being in touch with those who can arrange it. The rule here is the same as with liquor. Squeal on your friends if you love them and do not, literally, want to lose them. If you are a parent, be suspicious at all times and act on your suspicions *swiftly*. Indulging parents are totally disarmed in this matter. If they are regular drinkers or pot-smokers, they have little to say that can effectively restrain their children. The claim that they can "handle it," often an exercise in self-delusion, is no guarantee, even if true, that their children can. What their children cannot handle are the effects of growing up in a chaotic household. Thousands annually try to put their lives together in ACOA chapters (Adult Children of Alcoholics). Many more never do.

One has a responsibility to see that one's body is not drink- or drug-sodden. That responsibility extends to the bodies of others. A terrible helplessness overtakes the spouse, the parent, the son, or the daughter of someone "with a problem," as we put it. Why can't the addicted individual see that he or she needs help? People with the courage to suggest such assistance to their friends or relatives sometimes pay a heavy price for it. Deep, cold resentment often meets their suggestion, even the permanent loss of friendship. Suggesting help, though, is well worth the try because a human life is at stake. The destructive behavior has to stop.

In the same way, the friends of adolescents and adults who show suicidal tendencies, or have spoken of it even once as an attractive option, are in a delicate position. They do not wish to betray a confidence. They think that speaking of their friend's dangerous mental state to someone who could help would be taken wrongly by the friend. So they live with their fears unspoken. That is not the way of friendship. Friendship takes risks. It is better to risk the loss of friendship than to stand at the graveside and say to oneself, "If only I had talked to someone, told someone what my friend confided to me." Parents above all need to be alert for signs of depression, withdrawal, or nonengagement. Suicide ranks third among killers of teenagers. It happens in the most well-adjusted families. Often the parents of suicides literally had no warning signals or none they recognized. But just as often young friends did.

A Network of Friends and Counselors

The premise in all this is that human life is a great good and that life in the body is much better than death. Sometimes our own friends, parents, or children do not think so. There may be times when even we do not think so.

A great resource continues to be available in today's world. We call it friendship. It cuts across all lines of age and sex. It is built on trust. The world is filled with people who are locked up inside themselves and afraid to trust anyone. It is a great thing to enjoy the confidence of another person. There is no way of telling who will trust whom enough to open up to the other, to tell all that is weighing on a troubled mind. Young people often fear to confide in anyone but other young people. They thereby deprive themselves of the wisdom or experience of persons who could provide genuine help. They feel they cannot trust any adults. Or they think that no one could understand wanting to be dead except another person who feels the same way. However, it is no breach of trust but the barest proof of friendship when those who have been confided in take the burden outside the limited circle of friends. Often the confider wants to lay it on other, broader shoulders, hoping (even while swearing the friend to secrecy), that the confidence will not be kept. It is the same with a friend who is into drink or drugs. Turn her in. Squeal on her! A life is at stake.

All around us there are marvelous resources—psychologists, counselors, teachers, and clergy who listen as a way of life. The best of them do not speak much; they have the gift of hearing. These are the doctors of bruised hearts and injured psyches. The Spirit often dwells in temples of flesh that are perfectly sound while the temples of the psyche are shaky. A spiritual guide can have no point of entry, can even do harm, unless a doctor of the psyche has first provided entry by evoking trust. Amateurs at this art can often have a professional touch. Psychotics need psychiatric aid. Troubled spirits need a trusted friend.

The evoking of trust is a service of healing which we all need to provide to each other. It starts with hearing, not just listening. What is the other's pain? Is there enough trust for the sufferer to say to the listener, "Here is what I find intolerable about life. Has there ever been anyone in the world before me as weighed down as I? I doubt it. Will you share my burden with me? Will you listen?"

The Self-Made Who Worship Their Creator

The discussion above was about troubled people, some of whom are fairly sure they cannot stand another day of life in the body. They want the daily anguish of living to stop. No one knows how many of these people there are because they are not very big on telling their troubles.

Those about whom we know much more are the ones whose concern for their bodies assumes the proportions of worship. They are not the millions who think it is a good idea to stay in shape: joggers, people who work out regularly, amateur athletes. It is a good idea to keep Brother Ass in good condition, especially if sedentary work or rich food threatens to send waistlines ballooning. Exercise, if not gone after gluttonously, is the treatment the body needs. Physical laborers are not tempted to jog on their lunch hours. They've solved the problem another way.

The comfortably healthy in our day have a new temptation: paying divine honors to the temple of the body and none to the Spirit who dwells in it. The Holy Spirit? What minor spook is that, when the mystique of running is available to put one in touch with one's true self? Sometimes it puts a person in touch with some other runners' true selves, set wondrously free from bourgeois encumbrances like marriage.

Usually, the mystique of honoring the body is not so deadly that it breaks up marriages. It can work enough mischief by demanding of people that they become totally absorbed with their bodies in pursuit of health or beauty—muscle tone, a flat stomach, a face or figure that makes people turn and look. At first it is a harmless goal, even praiseworthy. The danger lies in the body's replacing the self as life's major concern.

It is a short step from there to disregarding the claims that others have on us. "You are not your own" (1 Corinthians 6:19b), Saint Paul tells us. "You have been purchased, and at a price!" (v. 20a). Paul is situating our true worth outside ourselves in the one who redeemed us. The sin of idolatry is to put the creature in the place of God or Christ or the Spirit of both. The creature may be money or sex or reputation—anything we can claim as ours.

The sorriest object of devotion is ourselves—self-made men and women who worship their creator. Worse still is the worship of a part of ourselves. "O woman lovelier than the swan, I shall not die for thee," wrote a nameless Irish bard. There is a fate worse than dying for a lovely woman. It is dying for *me*: my handsome looks, my marvelous encasement, my body. "I shall not die for thee," the Christian needs to say.

A. E. Housman wrote a rich and despairing poem in which he called the skeleton "the immortal part." To treat the mortal as if it has any genuine share in immortal properties is a bad bargain. In such a case another poet, William Johnson Cory, will be proved right: "For death, he taketh all away"—health, strength, beauty, all. The body favored as if it were not the Spirit's partner is the one that will have lost all reason to rise on the last day.

High-Powered, Life-Threatening Systems
In our day we hear of immense loss of life from handguns, not only as weapons of murder but as causes of accidents. That toll is bad enough, but it is nothing compared to the record compiled by our chief death-dealing instrument, the automobile. Thoughtful parents live in apprehension of the day when the symbol of young adulthood, the keys to the family car, must be turned over to their children. Leaving the complication of alcohol aside, the invention of the internal combustion engine did three things: it transformed the global economy, it gave power to the powerless, and it changed the pattern of family life in the industrialized world. It did more: in every corner of the globe, it left gaping holes in families who have lost a loved one, sometimes two or more.

Is there any such thing as *successful* driver education—a way of conveying to people of all ages that to be seated at the wheel of a car, bus, or truck is to be responsible for a potentially unguided missile of one or two tons equipped with combustible material? The skills for handling such responsibility are not nearly so widespread as licensed drivers. To engage in an animated conversation while driving—complete with gestures and direct looks into a seatmate's face—is to be a menance to human life. Not to know the basic law of momentum (M = mass x velocity) is to be a worse menace to human life. "No one ever told me I could go out of control cutting back in like that," is a tragic admission from a hospital bed.

Television ads are great offenders. When proceeding at high speeds, skilled test drivers, whose business it is to know the laws of physics, are never asked to give sixty-second lectures on these laws. Instead they parrot the copy written by advertisers, which gives the false impression that the mechanism of torque and balance can handle all road problems. *No* manufacturer can overcome momentum.

At certain speeds and in certain conditions, mechanisms can do nothing. Instead of being presented with that grim fact, we are shown braking systems on wet roads. This contributes to the popular mentality that there is no problem that a superior car cannot handle. There is a huge problem in the morality of driving, and ignorance of it is no excuse. The lass in her grave, the lad in his immovable brace for life can only be addressed with shame by the uninformed driver: "I did not know." Part of a life-protecting ethos is to know what a car can and cannot do, what a driver can and cannot do.

The weavers, the tailgaters, the dawdlers, and the light-jumpers are potential killers. They are probably not nearly so numerous as people who blithely admit to being poor drivers but take no pains to improve themselves or stop driving. These menaces need to take themselves off the road as a matter of conscience. A short-term measure would be to ask forgiveness in the sacrament of reconciliation for holding human life so cheap. The last sin thus confessed, according to the recording angel, was in 1913.

Bad drivers as a class happen to be the most numerous

threats to human life through inadvertence and carelessness. But the careless who threaten human life are by no means confined to the steering wheel. They are everywhere in our industrial society.

Happily, many people are charged with guarding the lives of others and do it well. Among these are health care personnel, those who manufacture cars, elevators and all sorts of machinery, pharmacists, baby-sitters, and bus drivers. The list is long. Every occupation on it is important. We all survive from one day to the next by a network of mutual trust. Centenarians make statements to account for their longevity that are partly serious and partly tongue-in-cheek. Their reasons for longevity should be headed by the life-protecting decisions of anonymous multitudes every day of their one hundred years.

A human life, our own and everyone else's, is a fragile thing. It should be guarded as if it were a temple of the all-holy God, for in fact it is.

The Morality of Preserving and Prolonging Life

The devout as well as more casual believers are prone to speak of the date of their death as something that is "in the hands of the good Lord." They are right, of course. But they may not realize that they themselves have much to do with setting the date by a lifetime of conscious choices.

An arterial system and a cell structure programmed in the genes are beyond anyone's control. Still, a strong faith in providence is no substitute for human responsibility. There is such a thing as accident or chance. To call it such is not to impugn the providential design. Jesus put the question once: "Do you think that these Galileans [whose blood Pilate had mixed with their sacrifices] were the greatest sinners in Galilee just because they suffered this? By no means!... Or take those eighteen who were killed by a falling tower in Siloam. Do you think they were more guilty than anyone else who lived in Jerusalem? Certainly not!" (Luke 13:2–5).

Jesus faced the mysteriousness of God's design and so must we. Pilate's cruelty, however, was responsible for the suffering in the first instance and probably someone's carelessness in the second. God will call us when God will call us, but we have no permission to hasten the day.

Must one stay alive as long as one can? How long must the living struggle to keep another person alive? These questions are qualified by what is meant by *life* as it gives clear evidence of ebbing. The issues are important and are daily becoming more so with the progress of science, medicine, diet, and labor-saving discoveries. Life expectancy rises in our culture with every decade.

The short answer about life is that it must be protected and prolonged whenever this can reasonably be done. A Catholic may not opt out of life to avoid suffering nor actively assist others to depart from life out of compassion. Conversely, there is no divine mandate to suffer if it can be avoided and no moral necessity to hold onto life by whatever means when death is certain.

Is death ever certain? It often is. If pressed to do so, doctors can confirm a person's intimation of impending death. They can frequently predict death's certainty. Some of us will have a measure of freedom about the time of our death. We see in some who seem close to death the will to live and in others the will to die, although many do not have the option. But the will to live can be effective for a matter of days or even weeks and months. Conversely, some appear quite consciously to "let go."

The ancient oath of Hippocrates pledges physicians to the preservation of life, not to its termination. Most are faithful to that pledge throughout their lives. Some physicians in their dilemmas seek guidance from the ethics committees of the hospitals to which they admit patients. Others resist such committees. They view the idea of a hospital's operating on a set of moral principles as an attack on their professional judgment, viewing themselves as the ones to whom decisions about preserving life have alone been committed.

But medical-ethical judgments are increasingly difficult "calls." The problems posed by the possibility of prolonging life by respirators and the intravenous feeding of the unconscious are enormous. The distinction between ordinary and extraordinary means of prolonging life, which was helpful over many decades, is no longer useful. New medications, techniques of surgery, and mechanical contrivances have made the former dividing line a wavy one. Yesterday's extraordinary means is today's ordinary. Catholic morality makes dying persons responsible for the decision on whether to continue living by artificial means when death is certain. When their capacity to decide has failed, it falls to the persons closest to them to decide. Artificial, short-term biological life may not morally be forced on anyone, however frequently the practice occurs. Often families of the brain-dead or the irreversibly deteriorated make the decision to stop the useless prolongation by machine and find themselves thwarted by doctors fearful of a legal suit. Sometimes it will be a code imposed on hospitals by a maximalist ethic, often from a religious agency which fears involuntary euthanasia. Their maxim seems to be: "While there's breath there's breath."

In November 1988, Missouri's Supreme Court, in the case of a young woman in a coma for five years, ruled on the legal status of patients' advance expressions of wishes (sometimes called "living wills") regarding the termination of their feeding. The court denied legal status to such wishes and to similar ones from the patient's family or guardians unless the patient was imminently dying or suffering pain from the feeding tubes. Numerous states have passed laws governing the provisions people may make for ending medical treatment when they are terminally ill. Some statutes exclude artificial feeding and hydration from procedures that can be withdrawn, some include it, some are ambiguous, and some have already been limited by court rulings. At the heart of the debate is the distinction between "killing" and "allowing to die." The question is: On which side of the line should the withdrawing of feeding tubes be put? The Catholic position on active euthanasia ("assisted suicide") is that it is not permissible. A loved one's life of pain or discomfort may be difficult to watch but no individual has been given the right to terminate it. The church makes no pretense of comprehending the mystery of suffering. It says of it that it is redeemable in the mystery of the suffering of Christ in head and members.

One development in public morality that makes decisions about preserving life difficult is the changing view of the unwanted child. Until recently, society had been the arbiter of society's needs in this matter. But in cultures such as ours, where children have gone from economic advantage to economic burden and a woman's rights over her body are coming to be defined as sovereign, the question of the preservation of life before and after birth has acquired new dimensions. In some circles the Hippocratic oath is being redefined to mean the protection of life and the restoration to health of those deemed capable of "meaningful life." Previously, all life was thought to have meaning. This delicate moral question is by no means without nuance, although the whole Catholic tradition is on the side of sustaining life.

Catholic morality does not speak with a single voice in the matter of whether merely vegetative life, either of newborns or others, must be called human life and protected as such. It would be wrong to pretend there is a single voice. A Catholic consensus does exist, however, that everything must be done to maintain life at the edge. The condition is: if such measures do not impose an intolerable burden in pain or expense on individuals or families. It is families or dear ones, not doctors, hospitals, or churches, who have the say in the balance between benefit and burden. This is the case in theory, although often those responsible find it hard to make their right prevail. Technology has made it very difficult for people to die or be let die naturally. No medical or religious-ethical principle of life preservation can give anyone the right to impose a great financial burden on a family to sustain for weeks or months or years a life that is irreversibly headed toward death.

As to creating the conditions of life at its beginnings, Catholic morality is opposed to surrogate motherhood because of its firm view of offspring as the fruit of marriage. On *in vitro* fertilization by a husband, no Catholic consensus exists as yet. Papal theologians have lately written against it, saying that conception by a wife should come about only in the old-fashioned way. The immediate, wider Catholic theological response is not nearly so sure. It more generally makes the case that a married couple have a right to their own offspring and therefore a couple who cannot have children by the old-fashioned means have a right to beget their offspring by any other means possible. Importantly, Catholic gynecologists acting as religious ethicists are as deeply involved in these debates as moralists from among the clergy. The role of the ethicist committed to Christian values falls to those with the requisite learning and conviction. It cannot be confined to those who claim the mantle of philosopher or theologian, whether ordained or nonordained.

Medical-ethical problems are of intense interest to Catholics for at least two reasons. The transmission and cessation of life are essential to our existence; there can be nothing more basic. Catholic theologians, moreover, seem to deal with them with more rigorous arguments than ethicists of other religious persuasions. "Classic cases," doctors are prone to say, occur more often in textbooks than in real life. The intense interest in these questions can give the wrong impression that they are the church's chief concerns about life in the body. The paradox is that in our culture—apart from modern abortion practices— human life is dealt with very carefully in most of the difficult cases of life's beginning and end. Only on a day-to-day basis is life held cheap; in times of crisis it is valued.

That is why it seems right to stress in these pages the contempt for the body and the life-threatening lifestyles that are all around us. Medical-moral problems of birth and death are both important and interesting, but they take second place to the day-to-day challenge of sustaining life in the body.

7

Lying, Stealing, and Cheating
Versus
Keeping One's Word

The United Negro College Fund features in its appeals the watchword, "A mind is a terrible thing to waste." That powerful statement is correct beyond any doubt. A mind in itself is not affected by color but the tragedy is that young blacks, Native Americans, and poor whites are more subject to the possibility of having their minds wasted than others. The waste in question is that a mind can go unused, unchallenged, and specifically, uneducated.

A mind can be wasted in other ways—for example, by the cocaine indulgence of well-educated yuppies or the beer swilling of people in all social groups but especially among college students and the working poor. A mind is a terrible thing to waste by confining its potential to money-making or to the power over others that money-making brings.

There are many ways, in other words, to destroy an intellect. Not getting to college when one would profit by it is regrettable but it is by no means an unrelieved tragedy. There are worse.

A mind is a terrible thing to twist, adulterate, or put to perverse use. Lies do this to the mind. Theft does the same. Detraction and slander can dull the edge of this sharp instrument. The mind is made for knowing the truth and shaping it into words to announce it. To say what you mean to do and do it is the way of virtue—unless, of course, you promise harm to another and carry through on that promise.

Honor: False and True Meanings

All kinds of terms can describe the practice of honesty or keeping one's pledged word: *integrity, honor, uprightness of character.* To be integral is to be whole, a complete human being. The word *honor* has unfortunately been used to describe certain false codes of conformity that feature exaggerated display and even vengeful pursuit. In his *Don Quixote*, Cervantes took delight in spoofing the chivalry that had prevailed a few centuries earlier and that had left lingering traces of absurdity around the Spanish countryside in his day.

Little good can be said of the twisted Sicilian brand of honor known as *omertà*, a code of getting even in blood feuds by taking life for life. But at its best, honor is a high human value. It means doing the decent, the noble thing. It involves acknowledging the sublimity of one's own humanity and that of everyone else we serve. "You can always count on Jane (or John) to do the honorable thing," is high praise on the lips of a Christian. "Honor bright!" is a phrase not heard much any more. It is a pledge to keep one's word.

Biblical Understandings of Honesty

"You shall keep away from anything dishonest," the Bible says (Exodus 23:7). And in a nearby verse: "Never take a bribe, for a bribe blinds even the most clear-sighted and twists the words of the just" (Exodus 23:8). Says the biblical collector of moral axioms, "Lying lips are an abomination to the Lord, but those who are truthful are his delight" (Proverbs 12:22).

No philosophical rationale is provided for statements like this in the Bible, no epistemology that explains why tongue and mind must always conform. The assumption is that the liar is a diminished human being, that no satisfactory way exists to do business with a cheat or a deceiver. Jesus, a Jewish moralist in the classic mold, taught: "Say 'Yes' when you mean 'Yes' and 'No' when you mean 'No.' Anything beyond that is from the evil one'" (Matthew 5:37). The anonymous author of the collection known as James said the same (5:12b).

It pleased the evangelist John to call Jesus simply "the truth"—meaning God's truth, one that had indisputably come from God (see John 14:6). Saint Paul took it as a given that God is faithful to every word God ever uttered. Because this is so,

Jesus Christ, whom Silvanus, Timothy, and I preached to you as Son of God, was not alternately "yes" and "no"; he was never anything but "yes." Whatever promises God has made have been fulfilled in him; therefore it is through him that we address our Amen to God when we worship together (2 Corinthians 1:19–20).

Much later, Shakespeare could say in a sonnet that "love is a fixèd star." But the whole biblical record is that God and the Christ of God are *truth*, the one fixed point in our moral universe.

Newman and Kingsley: On Catholics and the Truth

For the January 1864 issue of *Macmillan's Magazine*, Charles Kingsley, a clergyman, novelist, and poet, wrote a review of volumes seven and eight of James Froude's *History of England*. The authorship of the review was identified only by Kingsley's initials. Upon its appearance, someone sent a marked copy of it to the great English convert to the Roman church (later a cardinal), John Henry Newman. On 30 December 1863, Newman wrote from the oratory at Birmingham to protest a passage from the review:

> There, apropos of Queen Elizabeth, I read as follows:— "Truth, for its own sake has never been a virtue with the Roman clergy. Father Newman informs us that it need not, and on the whole ought not to be; that cunning is the weapon Heaven has given to the saints wherewith to withstand the brute male force which marries and is given in marriage. Whether his notion be doctrinally correct or not, it is at least historically so."
>
> There is no reference at the foot of the page to any words of mine, much less any quotation from my writings, in justification of this statement.

Kingsley was shown Newman's letter by Mr. Macmillan. He acknowledged to Newman that he had written the review and said that a passage in Newman's sermon entitled "Wisdom and Innocence," published in 1844, was "expressly referred" to in what he had written. Newman, by letter to Kingsley, said he was amazed that he himself could have been the author of the opinion and that Kingsley was "referring generally to a Protestant sermon of mine...published by me, as Vicar of St. Mary's...." He also wrote to a friend that "the *onus probandi* [burden of proof] lies upon [the two gentlemen responsible for so grave an inadvertence]." The friend conveyed the above comment to Kingsley as he was probably expected to do.

This communication netted from Kingsley a letter prepared for the editor of *Macmillan's*. The letter recorded Newman's "denial of the meaning which I [Kingsley] have put upon his words" and Kingsley's "hearty regret at having so seriously mistaken him; and my hearty pleasure at finding him on the side of truth, in this, or any other matter."

Newman complained about the latter quoted phrase and an earlier one, which suggested that as a master of verbal fencing,

Newman knew as well as any person living how to insinuate a doctrine without committing himself to it. So Kingsley withdrew these offending phrases. But the published letter of the February 1864 issue retains the phrase that Newman chiefly objected to—namely, "his denial of the meaning which I have put upon his words."

In a reflection on the above exchange, Newman recorded for his own satisfaction one of the better-known imaginary conversations of English letters:

> Mr. Kingsley relaxes: "Do you know, I like your *tone*. From your *tone* I rejoice, greatly rejoice, to be able to believe that you did not mean what you said."
>
> I rejoin: "Mean it! I maintain I never *said* it, whether as a Protestant or as a Catholic." Mr. Kingsley replies: "I waive that point." I object: "Is it possible! What? Waive the main question! I either said it or I didn't. You have made a monstrous charge against me; direct, distinct, public. You are bound to prove it as directly, distinctly, publicly;—or to own [that] you can't [prove it]."

The correspondence between Newman and Kingsley led to a pamphlet by Kingsley entitled *What, Then, Does Dr. Newman Mean?* and then to the somewhat better-known response to the pamphlet by Newman entitled *Apologia pro vita sua*, written at high speed by May 1864. The bulk of Newman's book is a "History of My Religious Opinions" up to 1845 in four chapters, culminating in this statement: "From the time I became a Catholic, of course I have no further history of my opinions to narrate."

But Kingsley's main charge—that of the Catholic clergy's careless regard for the truth—still rankled the priest of the Oratory. So he appended a thirty-page note, the final part of an appendix, on "Lying and Equivocation." It reviews the way that the virtue of truth has been dealt with from the fathers of the church down to certain mid-nineteenth-century Catholic and Anglican theologians. The note is still well worth consulting. In it Newman recorded the widespread perception among Protestants that "the Catholic system, as such, leads to a lax observance of the rule of truth." Newman regretted that Protestants should think so, but he admitted that he could do nothing about it beyond documenting the consistent Catholic teaching that goes in the opposite direction.

At the present point in Christian history there seems to be little difference between the two major Western Christian traditions in the matter of respect for the truth. What used to be a lively debate between Protestant and Catholic thinkers about mental reservation, equivocation, and dissimulation is such no longer. The observation of Saint Paul in a much more general vein can be said of both traditions: "All...have sinned and are deprived of the glory of God" (Romans 3:23). When Sissela Bok, a Protestant, wrote her modern classic *Lying* (1978) and when John Noonan, a Catholic, wrote his *Bribes* (1984), neither work had a confessional slant. The guilt is spread about quite evenly.

Why Catholics Lie

Why do Catholics lie, whether they do so in greater or less measure than other Christians? In small matters, the lying would seem to be chiefly because of a lack of courage. Let us suppose that one has failed to meet an obligation, namely, to do as one said one would. The easiest way to save face is to lie. In the short run, the individual supposes, the other person will think better of me. This may be the case until it is discovered that one is a chronic liar—first a defaulter and then a prevaricator.

We lie for other reasons. It is an easy way to gain an advantage over others when earning the ascendancy over them we crave proves difficult. Lying shifts the blame and succeeds in deflecting the immediate censure. It makes other people think less well of those about whom we lie. Our hope is that people will thereby think better of us. But once the lie is discovered, the moral censure descends where it belongs.

Lying is a moral climate. It is in the air around us. Some people were made to pay a heavy penalty in youth for their infractions of the truth. Others never were. Taking a hard line on lying is not easy when you have been lied to much of your life. Those who have seen one parent consistently resorting to deceit in self-protection because the other has no taste for the truth have much to overcome. Consistent adherence to the truth requires courage. One needs to be schooled in it. A person who has regularly experienced lying as a response to life's challenges will not easily know how to treasure truth as a value. But sometimes a person raised on a diet of deceit will rebel against the lifestyle of lying in order to escape that madhouse for an ordered universe.

"O, what a tangled web we weave, / When first we practise to deceive," Sir Walter Scott wrote in his poem "Marmion." An obscure political essayist, Algernon Sidney, reminds us that liars ought to have good memories. There is a rich folk wisdom on the subject. What it comes down to is that no one trusts chronic liars, who after a while lose all capacity to trust themselves.

Do not mistake a habit born of weakness nor residing regularly in a world of fantasy for the kind of lying discussed here. Neither of these is the same as the lying that comes from a profound disdain for reality when adherence to reality's rules is going to prove inconvenient, frustrating, or costly. The disdainer of truth's demands, the liar, creates a private universe in which brute facts are trimmed, enlarged upon, or set aside entirely in the interest of some short-term advantage. When facts do people's private bidding, they lose their relevance as facts. The human mind has been robbed of its capacity to deal with the reality that is and has been made to create a world that is not.

Is there any hope for the liar—not the pathological liar who is seriously ill but the ordinary liar who takes regular shortcuts out of tight corners? There may be. The enormity of the offense sometimes comes home to such a person when the lie is punished surprisingly and fittingly: by a lost job, by the forfeited respect of children or peers, by a suit in court. Chronic liars sometimes come to their senses for the first time when they hit bottom.

Another kind of liar merits our pity more than our censure. This one knows how bad a given situation is but cannot tell the truth because of the pain it would bring to others. He or she therefore puts the best face on things—forever. An optimism of this sort shortly becomes an exercise in cruelty. To keep saying, "Don't worry, everything will be all right," when the next step is family insolvency or an external censure like bankruptcy is downright destructive. Clinging fast to a dream world requires no courage. It can help to make one universally liked. Facing the truth is the hard thing—a repulsive alternative. The truth brings great rewards in the end, but in the short run it makes terrible demands on those who love it. That may be why the evangelist John had Jesus say of himself, "I am...the truth" (14:6). Jesus knew how much the truth costs and he was willing to pay the price.

Cultural Forces Against Honesty

Today a powerful moral teacher is at work inviting us to think that the difference between truth and a lie is a matter of no consequence. This teacher is the television program, whether cop show or psychological drama. To describe either as shallow would be to invest it with profundity. The staple features are instant misunderstanding, irrational anger, and not so much a wavy line between truth and falsehood as no line at all. The characters lie readily and glibly, speaking just as insincerely as when they are telling the truth. Even the "good" types lie to achieve their doubtful ends. A viewing public that regularly digests the output of scriptwriters who betray no ethical sense whatever is bound to be affected.

A second powerful educational force is the conduct of public officials on the witness stand. Indictments for perjury, few as they are relative to the number of people in tight corners who give testimony, are distressingly frequent. A careful examination of the daily record of public testimony might yield the cynical view of financial and political life that, "they're all liars." The principle that prevails seems to be, "Let's get over today's hurdle. We'll negotiate the damage control tomorrow." One assumes that damage control will be achieved by lying to explain the original lie. With such models before the public—and the offenders are federal officials as often as they are state and local politicians—it is no wonder that people in the private sphere lie to cover much smaller-scale questionable deals. What used to be considered the *sin* of perjury—lying after one has taken an oath to God to tell the truth—remains the *crime* of perjury, whether the offender believes in sin or not. That this is so is one of the better features of our judicial system.

Mortal and Venial Deceit

Part of Kingsley's attack on Newman in the pamphlet he produced after their exchange featured the Catholic distinction between mortal and venial sin versus the virtue of truth-telling. A critique of the Catholic distinction was part of the Reformation outlook, which expressed horror at all sin indiscriminately. The Reformers considered the distinction of the Scholastics a laxity that was, in effect, a license to sin.

Catholic morality continues to teach that a generic, not specific, difference exists between the two types of sin. On the one hand, there is the option against God and neighbor so grave that it can destroy the bond of love and lead to eternal death (*peccatum mortale*). On the other, there is the offense that more readily gains pardon (*venia*) by daily deeds of charity without the necessity of sacramental reconciliation. The difference between mortal and venial sin, in other words, is one of kind, not degree. This is an important matter for the Catholic conscience, already overburdened in the centuries between the Council of Trent and the Second Vatican Council by the cheerful rigor with which moral theologians placed violations of the precepts regarding Friday abstinence and Sunday Mass attendance in the category of mortal sin.

Kingsley and the Reformers, however, had the better case—

psychologically if not theologically—with their insight that the "white lie" can easily be habit-forming. It can lead to a leap across the abyss to lying on a scale that deals death to the soul. A century ago Newman recorded the popular perception of Protestant clergy that their Catholic opposites dealt lightly with the truth. At the same time, Catholic clergy had a similarly poor view of the adherence of Protestant preachers to the Christian morality of sex and marriage. Both convictions flourished by generous helpings of ignorance and caricature.

Today—however those who are not Catholics are perceived—Catholics in our morally ambiguous society are not hailed for their love of truth. They are thought to be neither better nor worse than the general run.

In fact, Catholics may have a better *or* a worse record than the wider population. God alone knows. The fact is that Catholic religious leaders who write and speak publicly feature a moral agenda—weighty matters, all of them—other than the importance of telling the truth. This makes it impossible for the Catholic populace to say, "As is well known, we are distinguished among the religious traditions by our devotion to the truth." The testimony of confessors over fifty years of age, the men who have forgiven Catholic sinners in the sacramental forum by the hundreds of thousands, might well be that self-accusations of grievous lying and deceit are uncommon relative to the venial sins against the truth they have heard confessed. It could make one think.

The Lie That Strikes at Another

When we lie, whether in word or deed, we do an injustice. But injustice is the essence of all sin. It holds back from someone, or some ones, what is their due. People have a right to their possessions. A company, a public trust, or a parish has a right to its earnings, to donations given to it in good faith. The fact that public moneys exist in very large sums does nothing to set them free of public ownership. No one gains a right to lie or cheat or steal because it is commonly done in certain situations. Or because the dishonesty is scarcely detectable. Or because an impersonal owner will not feel the loss.

Detraction and Slander

People have a right to more than property. They have a right to their good name, which is their most cherished possession. A sum of money or a stolen object can be returned or compensated for. Reputation once damaged cannot so easily be restored. We belittle others usually as a means of promoting ourselves. We mistakenly think that if we set people low in public regard we will somehow thereby be esteemed higher. The fact that it never works that way discourages no one.

Envy is our desire to have what others possess—property, reputation, friends, even a spouse. Jealousy, by distinction, is a pathological self-regard. The jealous individual looks within and wants nothing taken from the self or the self-image in the direction of anyone else. Envy and jealousy as emotional states, or feelings, are corrosive to the individual. At the same time, they inevitably seek expression in ways that are harmful to others. A festering state of mind and heart is bad enough. The damage done seldom stops there. Envious or jealous persons reach out to do injustice to others because they think that less than justice is being done to them. Jealous individuals may wish to bring others low in public esteem out of sheer spite or hatred. They usually justify their behavior, finding reasons why the "truth" about another must be spread abroad. If the damaging statement is in fact true, it is considered *detraction*. If it is a lie and known to be such, the word is *slander*. *Libel* is slander proved at law.

The human tongue has been described as the only tool that grows sharper with age. When challenged about their malicious gossip, people may respond, "It's true, and if she were here I'd say it to her face." That is a way of saying that they would cheerfully add insult to their injury of the absent.

A Washington *grande dame* deep in the political life of that city was reputed to have had a hemstitched pillow that said, "If you can't say anything nice about people, come over here and sit by me." Detraction—or at its gentlest, belittling—is a sin that most of us are prone to. We hear a name in conversation. We have to cite a character flaw or a foible—some tidbit that the assembled company may not have heard. Silence is called for in such circumstances. We bear no burden so heavy in our little piece of information that it has to be laid down for relief at every opportunity. If the person's weakness must come to light, it ultimately will. We have no obligation to hasten the process. And we have a serious obligation in justice *not* to.

Only when testimony to a person's character is required of us—in serious matters like a recommendation for or against employment—are we allowed and even obliged to disclose our experience of that person. The usual course of character assassination, sometimes mild but more often vicious, goes along other lines than the obligatory disclosure. We pass along what someone else has said of another for its mere amusement value. Anything for a laugh. But the person we report on is diminished by our action and so are we. We do not rise very high by climbing on others, least of all when we have brought them low in the first place.

Stealing and Cheating

To steal or to cheat is to lie in deed or act. We spoke of theft at some length in the fourth chapter. Such actions violate justice because they appropriate what is not one's own, depriving the rightful owner in the process. People steal (and sell) examinations, as is well known. They do it to get promoted on a police force or pass the state bar exam or graduate from college. Often the pressures are intense. The candidates may be desperate. They think of the cost of failure to themselves in salary, position, or time and they do not want to pay that price. They do not ponder what the cost of cheating or stealing will be to the integrity

of their personhood—forever to have been a thief, whether publicly branded one or not. "He profited by taking what he had no
right to. He stole from others the job, the class rank, the promo-
tion to which they were entitled. He was made in God's image
and baptized into Christ Jesus, yet he forfeited the truth for a
lie."

Such dishonesty can be repented. Reconciliation with the human and ecclesial community and with God is always a possibility. In only one case may reconciliation not come about, that
is, when one opts to live in darkness, to flee forever the light
that is Christ.

"Her Word Is Her Bond"

We say we will do a thing. Saying so is easy. Then sometimes
we do the thing we promised and sometimes not. When the implications of the commitment we made come home to us, we
may welsh on it. We usually do this by not getting back in touch
with the one to whom we made the commitment. Some people
borrow and are never heard from again. Of these, many intended at the time to repay. A few never meant to. Their spoken or
written word does not commit them to a thing. It is a device to
deliver them from temporary embarrassment.

In the phrase "Her word is her bond," a bond is a writing under seal by which a person binds herself or himself to pay a certain sum by a certain day. For some people, no written paper or
seal is necessary. Their word binds them firmly. They know
they have to keep it, and they do.

Many nonreligious people have a code of personal honor in
matters like this, even when the religiously active do not seem
to. How explain this? Is Jewishness or Christianity, specifically
Catholicity, of no influence here? Often it seems that the word of
the good pagan who was raised in honor is to be preferred to
that of the slippery believer.

A sense of honor for the Catholic comes with a family tradition of fidelity to one's baptismal promises. They are renewed

each year in the Easter liturgy, but that is only the formal commitment. The actual renewal is a matter of daily speech in home,
office, school, farm, and factory: "Do you reject Satan?...And all
his works?... And all his empty promises?" "I do." The devil is
the father of lies from the beginning, Jesus said. He covers none
of his bets, redeems no pledges, follows through on no commit-
ments. Satan's words are only words. Sometimes they are evil,
damaging words. Jesus' words are truth. Truth is a hard-bought
thing. It is not available anywhere at discount rates. You open
your mouth, say what you mean or what you mean to do, and
pay the full price.

The Bible tells us repeatedly that God is to be trusted. The
people who knew Jesus said the same: you could count on him.
A faithful follower of Christ is someone you can rely on. There
is no bluff there, no fakery, no deceit. Words are as good as
deeds. Living close to people like that is a paradisal existence in
a land called Truth.

8

How to Succeed in Business by Really Trying

The movie *Wall Street*, released in fall 1987, tells about a financier named Gordon Gekko (Michael Douglas) who fought his way to the top in the brokerage business without inhibition or scruple. Gekko is a caricature, of course. So is Bud Fox, the young comer, and Lou Mannheim, the incorruptible veteran of many a financial-district war. Hollywood is better at cartoons than portraying in-depth characters or expressing any kind of lasting ethical message.

As cartoon, though, the film is highly successful in conveying what one reviewer (John Gross) called the ultrafast megabuck which has succeeded the fast buck: "Unheard of sums of loose change slosh around the world; predators devour corporations that once seemed invulnerable; juniors take for granted salaries that not so long ago very few of their seniors could hope to command." The hostile takeover, buyouts, and trading in junk bonds is daily news fare. Starting with Black Monday in October 1987, the newspapers provided enough documentation to render the movie's portrayal a fairly accurate one.

At about the same time, the English dramatist Cheryl Church-ill saw her play, *Serious Money*, come to New York after a London run. It deals with the legal changes that ushered in deregulation in Britain in 1986. The play takes on capitalism in a way that *Wall Street* does not, and indeed no U.S. film could afford to. In *Serious Money*, the young traders are depicted as the stamping, arm-waving screamers of obscenities that they are, by no means an improvement on the London Stock Exchange world of an earlier day. The show ends with the entire cast chanting with frabjous joy, after the Conservative Party government has been returned to power, "Five more [seven-letter-word] glorious years."

Tom Wolfe, the journalist and social commentator who gave us an account of the astronauts, *The Right Stuff*, produced a couple of years ago a novel that he titled *The Bonfire of the Vanities*. It is not about Savonarola and the piazza of Florence, as you might expect, but about an investment banker who is the son of a Wall Street lawyer. This banker comes to think of himself and a few hundred others like him as the "Masters of the Universe," a phrase he takes from his daughter's plastic set of Norse gods. The man's small son asks him at one point what bonds are and what trading in them means. His mother volunteers, uninvited, that trading in bonds means keeping a few crumbs from each slice of the cake. The difference is that in her illustration there really is a cake.

The New Greed

In a way, it is too easy to leap on the new breed and pummel it—those "well-educated white young men," in Wolfe's phrase, "baying for money." Often they are *not* very well-educated, having merely attended law or business school. But they knew what they wanted, and they headed for the canyons south of Houston Street (in New York it's pronounced *How*-ston), So Ho. These veterans of war games in college dorms headed themselves resolutely, at age twenty-five, to become corporate raiders.

Some of the new breed went to Saint Paul's or Hotchkiss, then to Yale and the Harvard Business School. Many of them are recent alumni of some School of Utility Cultures, Inc. (the invention of the other Tom Wolfe to describe New York University's downtown branch, where he taught and suffered), or, distressingly, Saint Thomas of Loyola.

About the latter crowd, it can be asked, "Is it possible to become an ace at the corporate takeover game and not miss a Christmas with your family visiting runaways at Fr. Bruce Ritter's Covenant House?" It seems to be. All perfectly aboveboard, you understand, so long as you do not ask too many questions about the height of the board. It is the American way in business. Clean hands. No grand jury indictments. No moral questions asked.

The American way in economics is coming to mean the servicing of more and more people who produce less and less. This country used to have products: farm products for the table, manufactured goods like the washing machine to make life less of a drudgery, heavy goods like coal, iron, and steel. While a few of our heavy industries survive they are flanked by a much-threatened petroleum market in Texas, Oklahoma, and Louisiana and a market for raw and processed metals that other countries produce more cheaply. Our foreign markets are in trouble not primarily because Asia and Europe cannot afford our products (that is part of it; the cost of U.S. labor is a major factor) but because they are beginning to find the work of other suppliers better than our own. It is still possible to make an honest living in U.S. manufacture and business, but it is getting harder. Among other reasons, the cities are not making tax concessions to manufacturers. They would much prefer the real estate taxes on high-rise buildings.

Stocks and bonds are not the only crap-shoot in this country. The same uncertainties attend large-scale contruction, housing, agriculture, and above all, small business. In the first three categories, you can be a big winner one year and up for a sheriff's sale the next. Hardworking business people and executives who

have three decades of performance behind them can find themselves without a job or a company within a span of three
months. Many homeless people, it comes to light, are not winos
or bag ladies recently sent into the streets from mental hospitals
but people who cannot pay the exorbitant rents in the cities.
Some homeless persons are still in the labor force, reporting to
work from their shelters every day.

All of these people whose futures are so chancy—whether they
are in high, low, or intermediate income brackets—have been affected by the new greed and are its primary victims. They are
victims of skyrocketing rents, conversions to condos, and out-of-
sight prices for homes. The banking, investment, housing, and
nonelected governmental profiteers have taken the country's
work force on a shoot-the-chutes ride in which they are at the
controls on the ground and run few risks themselves. They have
put the rest of us into one large "blind trust"—with tin cups and
pencils available to the losers (at regular market prices).

Whoever challenges the system—like the Canadian and the
U.S. Catholic bishops in pastoral letters on their countries' economies—is likely to be called a Communist and asked to go back
to Russia. The U.S. and Canadian bishops' pastorals delivered a
challenge not to capitalism, as is usually charged, but to the systematic abuses to which capitalism lends itself. These abuses are
not notably different from those to which corporate or state socialism lends itself. Capitalism versus socialism is not the issue
here. The persistent, well-orchestrated theft from the populace
by the rich who create the poor—who live at ease with the notion of an "underclass" that brings its troubles on itself—is the
issue.

Sometimes the rich are the military, at other times the members of the Party or the capitalist running dogs who estimate
their holdings at "just under a billion." For instance, early in
1987 one public servant who made his fortune in the private
sphere announced his retirement from a cabinet-level position
where he earned $99,500 a year during the previous eighteen
months. He missed New York, where people love the smell of

money. In Washington, power is what people are after. He could not foresee himself being interested in acquiring more power at those low rates of pay.

What, Then, Shall I Do?

What do you do about these matters if life in Jesus Christ means much to you, asking him through his body, the church, what your next move is to be? To be sure, you are quite powerless in the macro realm of economics but not entirely in the micro. Every time you hear the gospel read on a Sunday, you are hearing Jesus illustrating his points with stories from the economy of his time where the sharks ate the little fish every day.

The Roman Empire's client Jewish kings had been largely replaced as surrogates of power in Jesus' lifetime by a priestly aristocracy. It did Rome's bidding through taking temple revenues and collaborating with the empire in a system of tolls and taxes that bled the proletariat white. For whatever reason, this axis of throne and altar, of imperial administrators and temple priests, decided that it had to be rid of Jesus. Daily, Jesus had called the ugly system into question in favor of having all Jews submit to the rule of God. The threat which he constituted to the system had to be at the heart of the decision to do away with him.

Modern Christians who are moderately well-placed may be as powerless to solve their nation's ills as were the peasants of Jesus' time. However, the one luxury not open to these Christians is to fail to recognize the evils in which they play an unwitting part. Needless to say, Christians cannot for a moment play a witting or active part in these social ills. They have to identify the forces, the persons, and the parties that consistently make the rich richer and the poor poorer.

"Reading the signs of the times" is the way Jesus described the demands he made (see Matthew 16:3). He said that weather watchers in the agricultural and fishing trades had expert status but they seemed incapable of transferring these skills to analyzing

the fully intertwined economic-religious realities around them.
We are in pretty much the same condition. The male American
is an economic threat to the female, whether he wants to be or not.
She earns roughly 65 cents of his dollar, often for the same work.
It is a fact of life that has to be acknowledged. White people with a
minimum of education oppress people of color and those who
speak a distinctive brand of speech. Accents—the Cuban, the
European—can be overcome and have been; the abridgments of
freedom pass. But color and the circumstance of one's coming to
this land as a slave, by the consensus of the native whites and
immigrants from Europe, can never be overcome. This too is a
fact. The very system is oppressive. The honest follower of
Christ needs to acknowledge this.

Can individuals do anything about the gross inequities that
mark life in this nation, rich in resources and until lately in
achievements? The first step is to face the truth of the matter. So
long as we live with the myth of equal opportunity—in another
version, the myth of unlimited advancement—for those "willing
to work for it," we will perpetuate the inequities.

The myths are false. They are lies and need to be branded as
such. Twenty-four hours of total honesty by people who say
they believe in the gospel could shake the economic foundations
of this country. A lifetime of honesty by those who claim the
name Catholic would make an immense difference. The Catholic
body in the United States today is on the side of the oppressors,
not an even mix of the oppressors and the oppressed. It would
shortly become such, however, if black America began to see
that its hope lay in a Catholic body committed to evangelical
justice. But to dream such dreams is to make white Catholic fac-
es turn even paler.

So a little straight talk among us, an end to the mythologies in
speech that perpetuate our cruelties to races and classes and the
female sex, is a good way to begin.

Another early step is to deny from the housetops (how high
can a Catholic pulpit or classroom be?) that anyone can play the
U.S. economic game by its present rules with total moral impu-

nity. Not just indictable offenses are the moral hazard, such as loan-sharking, racketeering, mail fraud, and graft. The game itself is the hazard.

St. Paul once wrote in his first letter to Corinth (5:9–13) that he did not expect his believers to have nothing whatever to do with pagan worshipers of false gods. That would mean resigning from the human race. He said he was speaking of the way believers must deal with believers. Some comfort may be taken from this practical counsel. But not the wrong kind, not the type that says: "It's the only game in town. What else am I supposed to do?" The Catholic answer to that question is: Something other than the only game in town.

Getting Paid What You Are Worth

A person's worth should by no means be defined by his or her earning power. One's *labor* ought to be the clearest indicator of a just return. How can both of these statements be true without entailing contradiction? The market determines what a particular job is worth, but the market often lies. As Jesse Jackson asks, Where would segregated America be if black and brown people did not stand at bus stops early in the morning and late at night commuting to and from white America for an hourly wage? That wage is fixed by the dominant white economy. The two white salary earners who leave their home in the morning to net a respectable total income cry to high heaven if "the girl" raises her hourly wage by a fraction. Whatever the new rate, it is bound to be a tiny part of the couple's income. The credibility of all arguments that try to distinguish between the skilled and the unskilled, the educated and the uneducated, the lazy and the industrious breaks down in the face of the reality that all economies with a high standard of living depend directly on some people's having a low standard of living. The system cannot operate successfully any other way. The one is impossible without the other.

To get away, for the moment, from race as a factor, if we start to pay rural or small-town schoolteachers what we pay the doctors and lawyers and plumbers who are parents of the children they educate, the township's economy will shortly founder. The system nationwide is geared to expensive water mains and cheap education. It was decided long ago that years of college and in-service training are far less valuable than time spent in medical or dental school. Society has passed its judgment. The upper-echelon health-care professional, the undertaker, and the orthodontist provide essential services, in society's judgment. People who will work at the going rate can always be found for the "nonessential" jobs (as teachers, for example) because of their commitment to the work and their economic need.

The ranks of the poor in the United States have been increased by 30 percent since 1979. Although total employment grew by 8 million jobs, the number of jobs paying more than $14,000 a year declined by 1.8 million. All of the recent net growth in employment in this country has been in jobs paying less than $14,000; 60 percent of the net growth has been in jobs paying less than $7,000. Average black family income in 1987 was 56.1 percent of average white family income. Anyone who is committed to loving one's neighbor as oneself had better know these things and keep repeating them on a regular basis. The correlative moral obligation is to turn out of office, whenever possible, officials dedicated to the perpetuation of the imbalance.

Voting with Moral Conviction

In a rich country like the U.S., the rich create the poverty of the poor. The claim of helplessness in the face of mysterious economic laws is a fraudulent posture of those who hold power. Honest officeholders may be terribly handicapped in their attempts to bring about change, but the merchants of greed are beyond any doubt the cause of the poverty of 30 percent of the population. Curbing their predatory skills is not easy. In an important sense they "own" the elective offices of the land. Only the judiciary has by and large escaped the corrupting influence.

An honest citizen's first duty is *always* to vote in national and local elections and not to elect or return to office candidates dedicated to a preferential option for the rich. We have a euphemism for this option—"business interests." The interests of business are important and should be protected by good legislation. But protecting these interests is by no means identical with protecting the interests of the personally super-rich. The Catholic who is committed to social morality makes the effort to learn which officeholders are working for what interests or whom.

Exercising one's vote responsibly is a moral obligation. Many believers in the gospel who know this best do not have the liberty to carry it out. They cannot vote, or if they do it does not matter. It is possible to vote responsibly only if one has acquired a set of moral convictions to undergird the political choices one makes with the ballot. Where do these convictions come from? The study of the Bible under guidance is one place to arrive at moral values. But that guidance had better not be given by those of the political right, which thinks that God approves of all that right-wing governments and armies do. Hearing social morality proclaimed as the word of God from the pulpit is another place.

Catholic preaching is often silent on the moral issues that touch people's lives most closely, and for two reasons: first, the clergy are frequently not informed on issues of social justice, many of them having decided in youth that the gospel has profound implications for the individual and the family but none on a broader scale; second, some clergy who preach regularly to congregations other than the poor have been burned in the past by being accused of partisan politics. The accusations came when they mentioned neither parties nor persons but only moral issues of justice. Such a charge is unavoidable. The Catholic clergy nationally do not hesitate to run the risk of being called partisan if abortion is the issue, the unborn's right to life. They show no comparable willingness to endure the same accusations when the rights of the disadvantaged already born are at issue.

The Student View

The Catholic school and the school of religion are important places to convey moral convictions about the notion that America's business is business (in President Calvin Coolidge's phrase). An important consideration is that as school fees rise the students enrolled in Catholic schools will tend to come from homes less open to the demanding message of the gospel. Their parents are often on toboggans of consumerism; any talk of change is perceived as a threat to their precarious budgetary existence. Michael J. Fox's Alex Keaton may be the resident economic royalist in the home of his 1960s-style liberal parents, but young people today offer a more complicated picture than that.

The current situation might be described as a checkerboard. The idealistic students who are resisting the consumerist outlook of one or both parents are seated in a few squares. So are those committed to the Christian ideal that they derived *from* their parents. Both types of students are interspersed fairly thinly among the others, who are dedicated to getting all they can. Often this mentality is not spoken, not even thought out. But when it comes time to make decisions that mentality is what will govern the way great numbers will choose.

The adolescent fear of being different from one's peers in any respect has something to do with the secondary-school outlook. Some adolescents will mature in the direction of the sounder views that are available to them within or outside their homes, views they are incapable of hearing at this time in their lives.

First-year college students are not far removed in outlook from students a few years younger. However, once in college, they are already a select population. In the fall 1987 annual survey conducted by *Newsweek* through an educational research institute at UCLA, 210 thousand entering freshmen at 390 colleges felt that being well-off is an "essential" or a "very important" goal. At the same time, the lowest proportion of first-year college students in twenty years—only 39 percent—put great emphasis on developing a meaningful philosophy of life. Seventy-one percent, a new high, said that the key reason for their deciding to attend college was "to make more money."

Business continues to be the preferred career; a new high of 25 percent of the students named it as their choice. Interest in computing, engineering, technological, and nursing careers declined sharply in 1987, but an encouraging 8.1 percent of the students said they plan to become elementary- or secondary-school teachers. The latter figure was up from 7.3 percent in the previous year and was notably higher than the low point of 4.2 percent in 1982.

The first-year students' understanding of a career in business may be illumined by the desire of 77 percent to be "an authority in my chosen field" and of 45 percent to have "responsibility for the work of others." A soybean farm, a lumberyard, and a retail store that sells household appliances are all businesses. One wonders if they are thought of as such by those who wish to go into business. The students could well have management in mind—that is, the management of people, not the production and distribution of goods for human need.

"I Want the Business World—but Not Business"

When people describe themselves as being in the business world—not in finance, corporate management, or personnel but in business—what do they mean? The term *business* can include any of those three areas but normally it means the manufacture, sale, or distribution of items that people need or want. Usually it involves a product or a service that itself is a product.

A person who succeeds in business by really trying respects the integrity of all persons dealt with in the conduct of business and respects the integrity of both the product and the process. The product may be anything from perfume to heavy-duty machinery. It has a certain worth or market value—sometimes arbitrary. But the people who bring that product into existence have a worth that cannot be calculated. Even though a valuation of their labor is set, in terms of the sociology of labor and the present market economy, that is not the worth of the workers.

The lives of the workers—from the highest company official to the part-time custodial or maintenance person—are, in the strict sense of the word, *inestimable* in value.

Who can reckon the worth of a breadwinner at any level, whether a parent, a household supporter, or a maintainer of only oneself? It is impossible to reckon. Paying people what they will work for is easy to determine: advertise and interview. But paying people what their organized voice as a labor force has been able to command is a way of arriving at a just wage for them. In contrast, paying workers what a board of directors has decided is good for itself or for its top management in order to compete may be wildly off the mark of the workers' true worth, either their human worth or their worth in the business world. The inability or unwillingness of the U.S. Congress and/or administration to raise the minimum wage in 1988 and then again in 1989 above the current level of $3.35 (and that is the minimum for adults, not just 'teens in fast-food outlets!) is a sign of the dehumanization we are content to live with.

A problem is that people come to think they are worth the salaries they command or are awarded. They seldom are. Given the inflated or depressed condition of many of these salaries, it is impossible to be *worth* them. At the higher reaches of management or the professions, the fiction is such that people up there come to believe it about themselves in short order. This fantasy world has led to the salaries that graduates in certain fields will consider starting at. Often in today's inflated economy, graduates' expected annual salary is the total of what their parents earned in the first ten or fifteen years of their employment. When the parents themselves believe in this fictional system of worth by salary, the tragedy is compounded. In business the stage is set for the out-of-work thirty-year-olds or the dead-enders in their fifties who much prefer golf to what they have to do, if only someone would keep paying them a salary for playing golf.

Success in business may come as a result of hard work. Hard work is part of honest business, whether success comes of it or not. Climbing the ladder (if it is *that* kind of business) can become an absorption, destroying family life, human life, all that matters in life. One needs to determine how much of one's lifeblood, one's mental or emotional energies, is required for success or even survival in business. Sometimes a career change or a job change is necessary if the things that really matter are to prevail.

In any business—for example, a printing company in a city where much commercial printing is done—wise persons learn early the fragility of their line of work. A neophyte may think that it cannot fail, that it cannot have peaks and troughs. But it does. All life is seasonal, even a life that supplies basic commodities—like foodstuffs.

People who succeed at a life like this are those with a few basic ethical convictions. You stand behind your product. (Woe to those operators in seven figures who have no product!) You keep the word you give, even the word given in the telephone conversation farthest removed from a contractual commitment. You pay your bills on time. If you fall in arrears, you pay all your creditors something—regularly. You respect the persons you work for, however little some employers may command personal respect. You respect the persons who work for you or with you. You think of people's labor as their most precious commodity. You think of capital—essential though it is—as trailing far behind. The day you put money before people is your first day of failure in the business world. That is true even though the balance sheet never looked so good.

The Business of War

This small book may thus far have struck some readers as trivial in its overall concerns because the life-and-death issue of peace and war (whether with nuclear or "conventional" weapons—the latter a chilling euphemism) has not been touched on. Let us touch on this issue in what, it is hoped, is the most realistic way possible. It belongs in a chapter on business.

Military service can be honorable, especially in wartime. In peacetime it may be honorable, but the higher one rises in rank the greater are the temptations to compromise one's conscience. The making of wars is a business, a dishonorable business from start to finish. The politicans who make wars—they stop being statesmen the moment they plot one or promote the arms industry to sustain the economy—are a despicable crowd. The more so is this the case as they take every precaution to avoid dying or keep their sons from dying in the wars they make. Wars are made "to preserve the national interest." Sometimes that can mean survival as a people, a nation. The goal of national survival can lend to war a subjectively honorable character but not deliver it from objective madness. Most wars are fought to protect national business interests, which are seldom the interests of all the people. Often wars are fought to protect national pride, meaning here the *hubris* or arrogance of a few. The morally defensible war, especially one fought on distant shores or mountains in a nation's "defense" (an uglier euphemism still), is hard to identify. Careful accounts of the military engagements of the United States since World War II—accounts which were written well after the fact and which include analysis of two major "nonwars"— disclose what needless adventurism they were in pursuit of a wrongheaded foreign policy.

War is a business. Its few assured products are death and destruction for the many and profit for the few. But wars bolster the economy, it is said. They enrich some, it is true, and give short-time employment to those who survive them. These are very few relative to the total population. Most of the survivors are impoverished by war in ways far worse than economic. Wars are worth fighting because they achieve or maintain freedom, one hears. Freedom, though, can be struggled for and won in other ways. These alternative ways do little for a people's national pride. And the ways of peaceful struggle come at a cost to the nations that hope instead to profit by wars. Peacemakers are lauded, even given a prestigious prize at times, but ultimately disregarded or destroyed. Like Jesus, they are bad for business.

"Respect life" is a marvelous moral watchword. Translated, it means, "Fear greed. Flee lust. Hate war."

On 3 May 1983, the U.S. Catholic bishops produced a national pastoral letter entitled *The Challenge of Peace: God's Promise and Our Response*, in a third draft after as many years of revision. It is a careful document setting out the moral issues connected with peacemaking, the traditional arguments put forward to justify a people's participation in war, the production and control of armaments, and the obligations of individual and corporate conscience to resist when active participation in war is demanded of people by their governments. An apparatus of 127 notes provides a mixture of moral exhortations to peace and hardheaded discussions of the elements of the arms race.

The bishops' chief contribution is to alert both Catholic people and any interested parties (the Reagan administration was one such—it made a last minute personal appeal to each bishop to vote against the letter) to face the horrors of nuclear war. Regrettably, the bishops took the position that it is moral for a government to stockpile nuclear weapons as a deterrent to war so long as it is determined never to use them. The papacy through the Secretariat of State has the same view. This follows the conventional wisdom of public and military persons and the citizenry at large that there has been no nuclear conflict since 1945—date of the unspeakable hell of Hiroshima and Nagasaki—precisely because the two major powers know the extent of the nuclear arsenal of the other. This has never been proved. It can never be proved. It is, on the contrary, much more likely that the United States and the Soviet Union have not attacked each other in all-out war for reasons totally unrelated to the possession of nuclear arms.

Thus although conventional wisdom, the Vatican's Secretariat of State, and the bishops' letter have taken the line that stockpiling nuclear weapons can deter war, a better case can certainly be made that the likelihood of nuclear war is increased by the stockpiling of nuclear armaments in hideous quantities capable of making the globe uninhabitable many times over. In a referendum of 1987 the U.S. bishops, equally regrettably, did not depart from their earlier stand that nuclear stockpiling was morally defensible. This came in response to a signed statement of almost fifty of them asking for a change. Their original letter remains, nonetheless, a valuable if flawed moral resource.

Pope John Paul's encyclical *The Social Concern of the Church* of early 1988, which was released in the twentieth anniversary of Paul VI's *The Development of Peoples*, is the necessary complement to the pastoral letter on war and peace. The pope states there that "war and military preparations are the major enemy of the integral development of peoples." He finds the Soviet Union and the United States each guilty in its own way of "a tendency toward imperialism." This conclusion was fiercely attacked by conservative critics. It could only have been arrived at by a disinterested moralist who had a stake in neither power bloc. The letter judges harshly both Marxist collectivism and liberal capitalism, singling out for special condemnation the "all-consuming desire for profit" and "the thirst for power...at any price." The pope urges the superpowers to turn away from neo-colonialism and confrontation that bring about "wars of proxy through the manipulation of local conflicts."

Succeeding in business as a Catholic committed to Jesus Christ is a matter of really trying: trying to escape being sucked into a money machine, an investment machine, a war machine. They are all three the product of the same manufacturer whom Jesus once called a liar and the father of lies from the beginning (see John 8:44).

9

Conclusion

Most Catholic moral teaching is as clear as it was when Jesus and his disciples enunciated it. Changes in patterns of human living have modified it somewhat. So have the applications of law, philosophy, sociology, and economics to gospel axioms. But the responsibility to live at our human best in God's image, which is at the heart of all morality, has not changed.

The behavior or conduct of Christians is a matter of acting humanly—in concert or community, not alone—as disciples of Jesus. He was no voluntarist in morality, saying simply, "Do it because God commands it" or "because I say so." He challenged people to discover, in the context of their lives, what God would have them do by reflecting on the oldest and solidest traditions in Israel's Scriptures. This "doing the Father's will" that he enjoined proved without exception to be what was best for them. It was in every case what contributed most to their happiness. The paradox of Jesus' teaching was that choosing in favor of others brought the greatest long-term satisfaction: to one's community, to one's family, to oneself.

We have no record in either testament of Scripture of a morality that is purely individual. It is always social. Its implications for others go concurrently with its implications for the individual who chooses. The Bible is at the same time never committed to the emotions or the will or the two together as the sole locus of decision. There are always reasons of the head for or against a line of conduct. On the basis of these reasons one makes a choice. They can be eminently good reasons or just as readily bad ones: the noblest unconcern for the self or the lowest motives of self-interest. Passion, ambition, and covetousness, or conscience, altruism, and duty may enter in. But there are always reasons.

Jesus knew that God had implanted in the human mind the capacity to tell good reasons from bad. That is why he was so firmly set against hypocrisy. It gives good reasons for bad actions. People of today, especially young people, tend to put sincerity high on their list of virtues. They could hardly do better. The danger attending this lofty commitment is almost the opposite of hypocrisy: giving bad reasons for bad actions. When this bogus sincerity is elevated to the level of moral principle, Jews say in exasperation, "*Hitler* was sincere!" That is not dark humor but the profoundest of ethical observations. It will not do that your reasons for acting are *your* reasons or that you are faithful to them through thick and thin. Whatever your reasons for acting, they must be right and not wrong reasons, genuine and not perverse, true to your best interests and humanity's and not false to them.

One is not an alarmist to say that the morality of many Catholics in North America is fairly far removed from the expectations of Jesus and the gospel. Such may also be the case in Europe and parts of South America. That is hard for North Americans to judge, just as hard as for Europeans to judge the peoples of the Americas. All of us, however, whatever our culture, can have a measure of self-knowledge of our own moral stance.

If one looks for the *conditions* that contribute to the wide gap between North American Catholic profession and Catholic living, they are not hard to identify. Conditions are attendant circumstances, by no means the same as *causes*. The conditions of immoral behavior are easy to list. They include consumer goods in long supply and an advertising industry that more and more loudly sounds in the tattoo that happiness comes with having more and more of those goods; the identification of sense pleasure with happiness, relative to which little else promises much of a return; the breakdown of family life, however one spells it out in its causes; the sacrifice of public rights to private rights to the point where the latter become all-important and the former approach zero; the exchange of facing life's realities for a flight from them through resort to dreams or depressants, whether in a ghetto without hope or a suburb fraught with bla-ah. It is easy to compile such a catalogue because the components are a given. The question is: Can people who say they are disciples of Jesus resist the conditions of an immoral because an inhuman life that are as real to them as the air they breathe? In other words: Is Catholic morality possible in the technological West in the closing years of the twentieth century?

The starting point of an answer is to recall that Catholics are not alone in resisting the conditions of the death of the soul. Some Jews and some nonreligious people are just as dedicated to the cause as some Christians, Catholic and other; so are Muslims in the United States almost to a person; likewise the increasing Indian and far-Eastern populations that come to our shores full of hope and armed with a stringent, ancient ethic. As the opening pages of this book pointed out, Jesus the heir of Israel's law, prophets, and sages provides motives and means to live a moral life that are unique. That moral life is potentially the possession of all who are human.

The cause of immoral behavior by Catholics as distinguished from its conditions is freely made choices. Such at least is true of those who live at a material level that can afford the luxury of choice. Their choices can escape the influence of grace and even be opposed to nature. Sin (the Bible in translation sometimes calls it "iniquity") is a mystery to us who are perpetually threatened by it. We nonetheless have enough experience of freedom and freely offered grace to know that we can overcome this evil force both within us and around us.

There has always been mental confusion over what it means to be moral. This confusion accounts for the largest measure of departure from morality's demands. Characteristic of the present age is the confusion in the popular mind over precisely what is right and what is wrong. The whole United States culture, which once thought it knew, is in a state of lamentable uncertainty. Feeling has so overtaken thinking that it is almost a heresy to suppose that one can do hard thinking about a right course of action. Good moral argument is almost a fugitive. When moral claims are put forward they are likely to be softheaded without the redeeming virtue of being pure-hearted. The public forums for discussion that different audiences attend to—television panels, talk shows and call-in programs on late-night radio, newspaper columns, editorials—almost never entertain a good argument (in the sense of a logical one) about a correct way of acting. You get shouting matches based on opposite understandings of terms, a constant begging of the question, an appeal to parallel cases, but seldom a demonstrative *argument*. Anyone who holds an ethical position with conviction, particularly if it includes infringement on a person's untrammeled freedom, is likely to be declared dogmatic or worse. "Worse" is holding to a "religious" agenda when in fact religion has not entered into the discussion.

This country has become fairly woolly-headed over what to do and why in order to live a fully human life, Catholics along with the rest. Can it ever get back on track? If the 20 percent of the population who declare themselves Catholics began to live the ancient ethical convictions of their church it would help. Ancient, mind you, not those recently and sometimes imperfectly developed. For a start, they must think of *themselves* as the church, not as the subjects of a body of moral censors who propose positions they "cannot go along with." These teachers are not the church. Catholics are the church, Christ head and members. Sometimes they must part company with that body of moral censors. More usually, they, the bulk of the body of Christ, must make a commitment to have no part or lot in lying, thieving, revenge, greed, sexual deviance, cruelty, or violence.

We know the influences that contribute to a lack of such commitment. We also know the influences of family, church, and educators—a code of behavior embodied in upright lives—that contribute to such commitment.

Catholics faithful to Christ and the gospel hold these truths, the fruit of clear thinking and arguing, to be self-evident:

•No one makes an ethical choice that affects only oneself; that is impossible; every decision has some effect on all others, starting with those immediately touched by the decisions one makes or fails to make.

•There is a long-standing way of living as a Catholic which is corporate, a life in and of the church; its exacting demands have consequences particularly for those of the household of faith; fulfilling these demands will at the same time result in the good of all others.

•The best standard that Catholics have for the other-oriented existence they are called to live is the happiness they would wish to experience themselves; this they will try to ensure for their neighbors, loving them as themselves.

•Gospel living requires that persons have those possessions they need for an honest and virtuous life; an excess of possessions is a threat to the happiness of both individuals and those around them; the truth has its roots in the conscience question: How was the excess acquired in the first place?

•Persons have a title in justice to what they earn or inherit; some people are given gifts, but when the gift is large and the reason small, it is usually a bribe—for favorable action or silence.

•In this world somebody owns almost everything except sea and sky, which belong to all; people (and peoples) own what they own and no more; the seas and skys, and all that no one can lay a claim to, should be left as a heritage for all, no matter how much certain persons or impersonal corporations may dishonestly claim them as their possessions.

•People own land under a wide variety of cultural understandings, but basically the earth is the Lord's, entrusted to the human family over countless generations; it is rich but is plundered to poverty for the sake of short-term wealth; "Save the whales," "Save the seas," "Save the forests," "Save the atmosphere" are causes one expects Catholics to be deeply engaged in, not dismissed as a "liberal" aberration.

•There is much injustice in the world and many persons are victims of it; this does not give any the freedom to set the balance right by deciding what is coming to them and taking it.

•Each person has a right to enjoy the pleasures of sexuality in the measure she or he accepts responsibility for them; in practice that means being open to parenthood and all its long-term demands; no man or boy can claim he has a right to his own body and seek sexual satisfaction where he finds it without being ready for the consequences of his acts; no woman or girl has "a right to her own body" if that means seeking sexual gratification at will with no intention of accepting the consequences; people's sexual rights are real but they are strictly limited by their state or condition in life, namely, whether they are single or married, heterosexually or homosexually oriented.

•All must speak the truth and when questioned answer truthfully if the questioner has a right to know; liars hope to gain advantage over others, but in destroying their credibility they destroy themselves.

•None may seek profit or advancement at the price of another's reputation, position, or possessions; any progress upward at the expense of others is dearly bought; Jesus called such an exchange suffering the loss of one's own soul.

•It is grievously wrong to take a human life or notably to diminish its vigor, starting with one's own; anonymity does not lessen wrongdoing, as when people prosper by the wars they foment or support; neither do rationalizations lessen wrongdoing, as when people claim to see individual or social good in abortions and infanticides.

•Violence whether physical or psychic may not be visited on anyone, least of all when the attacker claims violence is a right to be exercised in response to the conduct of a spouse or child.

These truths may be self-evident but the dilemmas attending them are far from that. They can only be seen clearly by young and old alike if, as Catholics, they engage in constant dialogue about what is right and wrong, and *why*. The enemies here are the modern dogmas that if a thing feels good you should do it; that a course of action is permissible so long as it "doesn't hurt anyone"; and that everyone has an individual right to wl .tever one wishes in any matter not covered by the criminal code. The modern temper asks, "What kind of totalitarian God or church or society would wish to curb such a self-evident right?" The answer, of course, is a God and church and society that are at one in willing human happiness on the earth.

Anyone who has persevered through these pages may think that the writer lives in a dream world. He does, as the following survey should make clear. He has also taught undergraduate students in two universities, Catholic and State, for the past forty years, another kind of dream world.

In March 1989, the Gallup Organization conducted a survey on "The Religious Beliefs and Sexual Attitudes and Behavior of College Students." The poll was commissioned by the Christian Broadcasting Network of Virginia Beach, Virginia, a Pat Robertson organization. Interviewed were 539 randomly but representatively selected students from one hundred accredited colleges. Forty-eight percent of the students said they were Protestants and 28.9 percent Catholics, with 23 percent of the total self-described as evangelicals or "born again" in a 19 percent/4 percent division. There were 2.3 percent Jews and .7 percent Muslims who responded, while 2.4 percent expressed a preference for Eastern religions. Eight percent said they were agnostics or "do not know" what they prefer; 2.3 percent claimed atheism as their religion of choice. Students in the first two years of college constituted 68 percent of the population and those in the last two years 32 percent. Those from the midwest and south, almost equally divided, were 57 percent of all those questioned; 18 percent were from the west, and 24 percent from the east.

Religiousness was tested exclusively by one question on the importance of religion in the students' lives, another on their recent church attendance, and a third on their habits as Bible readers. Questions on sex and family life were the only ethical ones addressed. Responses to the latter by evangelicals were notably more in the Catholic tradition than those given by other Protestants or Catholics. The young Catholics' views on the chastity, fidelity, and protection of fetal existence expected of them by life in their communion were sobering.

The majority of Catholic women said they would like to marry, have children, and work full time. But 20 percent said their concept of an ideal life would not include children; 11 percent said they would like to remain single.

Most Catholic students (75 percent) said premarital sex is not wrong [although one-quarter acknowledged not having experienced it]; 18 percent said it is wrong. A smaller majority (59%) also said they approve of living together in trial marriages.

Three-fourths (76 percent) of the Catholic students said it is right for a couple to divorce if the two are incompatible and don't get along well. About 10 percent said divorce for that reason is wrong, and 14 percent had no opinion.

However, 90 percent said it is "very important" for a married couple to remain sexually faithful. Six percent said fidelity is fairly important.

Catholic students were slightly more in favor of a woman's right to have an abortion in the first trimester (53 percent) than were students overall (51 percent).[1]

One is immediately curious to know if other aspects of Catholic morality such as truth-telling, scrupulosity about money, a horror of war, and a commitment to justice in society would net the same half-hearted responses. Do the young think their sex lives to be their own affair in a way that other areas of ethics are not? What reasons would they give or arguments would they propose in favor of the moral neutrality or moral virtue of the positions they favor? Have they, in fact, ever heard these questions argued or do they just talk about them among themselves and go off to college armed with a blanket of parental silence, pierced only by a smattering of reminders to abstain or to "protect themselves"? A full and free discussion of the Christian morality of sex and parenthood might well be a "first" for many who responded to the survey. Evangelicals at least have the Pauline thunders against "fornication" ringing in their ears to restrain them.

The same inattention to other ethical questions as to those of sexuality might prove to be the experience of most of the respondents. This would confirm anyone's worst suspicions that we are sliding into a morality of hearsay and feeling instead of an orally transmitted tradition on why wrong is wrong and right is right.

The Hebrew Scriptures speak of periods of moral anarchy in the land of Israel, when "every one did what seemed right in his own eyes." Judges on the bench and public school educators and clergy of all the religions are more and more frequently moved to put the question publicly whether this country may be in such a phase. There is a floundering everywhere. There seem to be constitutional inhibitions against taking a strong line against everything but murder, child abuse, hard drugs, and driving while drunk.

The churches are not inhibited governmentally in any way, only culturally. Their own timidity and embarrassment in the face of certain moral questions are all that keep them from preaching, teaching, and more importantly arguing their convictions. The Catholic church is normally fearless in such matters. By a cruel paradox, summarized in the French proverb about the better being the enemy of the good, Catholic opposition to abortion and any sex education that recommends contraception has effectively silenced the Catholic voice on all other questions—even on warmaking and the economy so carefully addressed by the bishops' pastorals.

This need not be. The church is made up of enough persons who have the convictions of Jesus that they can begin to resume speaking freely about all that the gospel commits them to. No zeal for a limited range of questions should hold them back. Their moral position is by definition countercultural. The Catholic voice for humanity and against the culture *must* be heard.

Notes

Chapter 1

1. David Flusser, "A New Sensitivity in Judaism and the Christian Message," *Harvard Theological Review*" 126 (1986).

2. G. Vermes, *The Dead Sea Scrolls in English*, "The Hymns," no. XVIII (Harmondsworth, Middlesex: Penguin, 1962,), p. 200; cf. Matthew 5:4–5.

3. See Krister Stendahl, "The Apostle Paul and the Introspective Conscience of the West," *Harvard Theological Review* 56 (1963), 199–215.

4. In C. C. Richardson, ed., *Early Christian Fathers* (New York: Macmillan, 1970), p. 195.

Chapter 3

1. Alan Donagan, *The Theory of Morality* (Chicago: University of Chicago Press, 1977), p. 7.

2. A.P. d'Entrèves, *Natural Law: An Historical Survey* (New York: Harper & Row, 1965), p. 17.

3. Ibid., p. 27.

4. Ibid., p. 43.

Chapter 4

1. See *Origins* 17 (October 8, 1987), 285–86.

2. See "The Teaching of the Twelve Apostles, Commonly Called the Didache," in C. C. Richardson, ed., *Early Christian Fathers* (New York: Macmillan, 1970), p. 174.

Conclusion

1. Susan L. Norman, ed., *CBN Summary of 1989 College Student Survey* (Virginia Beach, Va. The Christian Broadcasting Network (photocopy), p. 3 .

Suggestions for Further Reading

Books like this one

Kohmescher, Matthew F. *Good Morality Is Like Good Cooking.* Mahwah, N.J.: Paulist Press, 1987. Paper.

Lohkamp, Nicholas. *Living the Good News: An Introduction to Moral Theology for Today's Catholic.* Cincinnati: St. Anthony Messenger Press, 1982. Paper.

Smith, Joanmarie. *Morality Made Simple But Not Easy.* Allen, Tex.: Argus, 1982, Paper.

Books on specific issues raised in this one

Berryman, Philip. *The Religious Roots of Rebellion: Christians in Central American Revolutions.* Maryknoll, N.Y.: Orbis Books, 1984.

Curran, Charles L. *Directions in Fundamental Moral Theology.* Notre Dame, Ind.: University of Notre Dame, 1985. Paper.

Gula, Richard M. *Reason Informed by Faith: Foundations of Catholic Morality.* Mahwah, N.J.: Paulist Press, 1989. Paper.

Hanigan, James B. *As I Have Loved You: The Challenge of Christian Ethics.* Mahwah, N.J.: Paulist Press, 1989. Paper.

Holland, Joe and Peter Henriot. *Social Analysis: Linking Faith and Justice.* Rev. and enl. ed.; Washington, D.C.: Center of Concern, 1983. Paper.

Keane, Philip. *Sexual Morality: A Catholic Perspective.* Mahwah, N.J.: Paulist Press, 1978. Paper.

Kohn, Alfie. *No Contest: The Case Against Competition.* Boston: Houghton Mifflin, 1986. Cloth.

Meehan, Francis X., ed. *A Contemporary Social Spirituality*. Mary-knoll, N.Y.: Orbis Books, 1982. Paper.

Musto, Ronald G. *The Catholic Peace Tradition*. Maryknoll, N.Y.: Or-bis Books, 1982. Paper.

Raines, John Curtis. *Illusions of Success*. Valley Forge, Penn.: Judson, 1975.

Rush, Vincent. *The Responsible Christian: A Popular Guide for Moral Decision Making According to Classical Tradition*. Chicago: Loyola University Press, 1984. Cloth.

Simon, Arthur. *Bread for the World*. Rev. ed.; Mahwah, N.J. and Grand Rapids, Mich.: Paulist Press and Eerdmans, 1982. Paper.

Toton, Suzanne C. *World Hunger: The Responsibility of Christian Edu-cation*. Marknoll, N.Y.: Orbis Books, 1982. Paper.

Varga, Andrew C. *The Main Issues in Bioethics*. Rev. ed.; Mahwah, N.J.: Paulist Press, 1984. Paper.

Documentation

Walsh, Michael and Brian Davies, eds. *Proclaiming Justice and Peace: [Ten] Documents from John XXIII—John Paul II*. Mystic, Conn.: Twen-ty-Third Publications, 1984. Paper.

National Conference of Catholic Bishops. *The Challenge of Peace: God's Promise and Our Response*. A Pastoral Letter on War and Peace, May 3, 1983. Washington, D.C.: United States Catholic Con-ference, 1983. Paper.

_____. *Economic Justice for All*. Pastoral Letter on Catholic Social Teaching and the U.S. Economy, November 18, 1986. *Idem.*

The United Methodist Council of Bishops. *In Defense of Creation: The Nuclear Crisis and a Just Peace*. Nashville: Graded Press, 1986. Paper.